MIND YOUR THOUGHTS

...THEY COULD BE MORE POWERFUL THAN YOU THINK!

❦

SUSAN MCELLIGOTT MA

CHANGING THOUGHTS HYPNOTHERAPY

COPYRIGHT

All rights reserved except as permitted under current legislation. No part of this work may be photocopied, stored in a retrieval system, published, performed in public, adapted, broadcast, transmitted, recorded, or reproduced in any form or by any means, without the prior permission of the copyright owners.

Edited and Published by Susan McElligott 2021

DISCLAIMER

Every attempt has been made to change any identifiable details and the material used in the making of this book is intended for training and teaching purposes.

The stories covered in this book are drawn from both my own personal life challenges and my work involving real-life clinical cases. If any of the content has a similarity to your own story or if you feel it is about you, it is not intentional.

The strategies found within may not be suitable for every person or situation. My suggestion is to take what applies to you and leave the rest.

This work is sold with the understanding that neither the author nor the publisher is held responsible for the results accrued from the information in this book.

DEDICATIONS

This book is dedicated to the memory of my late mother Angela McElligott, who lived on this earth for 89 years and who, despite her own personal trauma, taught me the power of resilience and laughter. It is through her 'quirky' sense of humour that I found my passion for helping others to see the lighter side of life.

I would also like to honour my father, Ted McElligott, who lived for 52 years. He always believed in me, which helped me to develop the courage to embrace uncertainty.

Not forgetting my youngest brother, Ted Junior, who came into this world for 11 years and made his presence felt, by teaching me the value of embracing life through the eyes of a child, with wonder and curiosity.

Out of the darkness, let there be light.

ACKNOWLEDGMENTS

I wish to acknowledge my mentors from all over the world, who provide high quality professional training in the Art of Hypnosis.

Since I began my journey as a hypnotherapist over 22 years ago, I have been privileged to meet, in person, like-minded professionals who continue to share their skills. Their teachings have become a great source of knowledge towards providing the best possible care for my clients.

I give praise to the commitment and dedication of my fellow committee members of the European Association of Professional Hypnotherapists (EAPH), who have worked diligently to promote our work as clinical hypnotherapists in making a difference to peoples' lives.

I am grateful for the support under the tutelage of my clinical supervisor Dr. Alvina Grosu psychologist, who guided me through the difficult and challenging times while doing my masters in counselling and psychotherapy. Her patience and commitment is very much appreciated.

I especially want to thank the thousands of clients that I have worked with in a clinical setting, for the past 20 years.

Most of all, I want to thank the clients who have offered to share their stories for the purpose of helping others who may find themselves in similar circumstances. Their contributions have provided invaluable teaching tools and have become the foundation towards the creation of this book.

TABLE OF CONTENTS

Author's Note	xiii
Introduction	xv

1. THANKS FOR THE MEMORIES — 1
- The Trained and Untrained — 2
- Support Systems in Place — 2
- Sleep Deprived — 3
- Practice What You Preach — 4
- Communication Breakdown — 4
- Nightmare — 5
- I Can't do It — 7
- Somewhere Over the Rainbow — 7
- Laughter is the best medicine — 8
- Making her Voice Heard — 10
- Thanks for the Memories! — 10
- Making Movies and Home Entertainment — 11
- The Phoenix Bird Rises from the Ashes — 12

2. IT'S EITHER ME OR THE DOG! — 14
- Out of Sight, Out of Mind — 15
- Frozen in Fear — 16
- Flight with Fright — 17
- The Tangled Web of Family Dynamics — 18
- Hypnosis Leads the Way — 20
- Meeting her Younger Self — 21
- Root Cause — 22
- New Challenges — 24
- A Dog's Life — 25
- Losing the Fear — 27
- New Life New Path — 28

3. NOT DOGS AGAIN! — 30
- Sweet Rewards — 30
- The Sweetest Granny — 31

Building Trust	32
Setting the Stage	33
A Wise Old Dog	34
The Animal Kingdom	34
Out of the Mouths of Babes	35
Secondary Gains	35
The Grownups World	36
Facing the Fear	36
Therapeutic Chameleon	37
Teaching an old dog new tricks	38
4. TAKING THE BISCUIT	40
Disappearing Biscuits	41
His Story	42
The Hypnotic Trance	43
Caught in the Act	45
Secret Promises	46
What you Resist Persists	47
Unravelling the Mystery	47
Freedom at Last	48
5. BONJOUR KARMA	51
Killjoy	52
Unreasonable Expectations	53
The Student is Ready, and The Teacher Appears	54
Emotional Triggers	55
The Phoenix Bird Rises	55
Karma revisited	56
Lesson Learned	56
6. SHADOWS OF DOUBT	58
Revelation	59
Playing Games	60
Our Inner Critic	60
Pink Elephant	61
7. SILENT ANGER	62
Burning Rage	65
A Living Nightmare	65
Healing the Triggered Part	66

Labels	67
Finding a New Identity	68
8. BURDENS OF SHAME	69
Nightmare Reality	71
House of Horrors	73
Freedom at Last	73
Siblings Reunite	74
Struggling in the Abyss	75
Imprisoned by Thoughts	76
Earth Angel	76
Hope is Near.	77
Opening Old Wounds	78
9. DRIVING CONTROLS	82
Walking on Eggshells	83
Breaking Barriers	84
Slowing Down	85
Disengaging Fears	86
Releasing the Clutches of Grief	89
Responsible Choices	90
10. PULLING HER HAIR OUT	92
A Voice Unheard	93
Getting a Grip	94
Breaking the Silence	95
Guilty Secret Unveiled	95
No one is Listening	96
Shame on Me	97
Understood	99
11. HOME IS WHERE THE HEART IS	101
12. I AM NOT MY STORY	110
Lifting the Veil of Truth	113
Rewriting My Story	115
13. GROUNDING & HEALING ENERGY MEDITATION	117
Further Reading & Viewing	121

AUTHOR'S NOTE

This book aims to show you, the reader, how easy it can be to overcome any emotional challenges you may be facing in your life right now. When you change the meaning you associate to any situation, it changes the entire dynamics, and you will never be able to look at it in the same way again.

Grief and loss have been part of my life's trajectory, which has led me to explore the qualities and inner resources of a person, to discover what it takes to become a survivor in the face of difficult and challenging situations. It is through the trauma I have suffered in my own lifetime, that I am now able to shine the light on those who walk a difficult path. I cannot walk it for you, but I can walk it with you.

As part of my master's degree, I chose to study existential psychotherapy, which relates to the four basic dimensions of human existence: the physical, the social, the psychological, and the spiritual. My dissertation was to explore the lived experiences of end-of-life caregivers from these four dimensions. My research examined their own unique experiences and how they coped during distressing circumstances.

I have included my own subjective experiences as an end-of-life caregiver while looking after my own mother in her final years of her life, and I have described some of the challenges I encountered along the way. I would like to offer hope to those who find themselves in a similar situation.

My intention while writing this book, is to offer practical, useful learnings that may benefit you in some way, to make your journey through life that little bit easier.

The stories cover different emotional problems and include both professional and personal content. I hope you will find some parts of this book insightful and beneficial.

"Pain is inevitable, suffering is optional." ~ Dalai Lama

Susan McElligott M.A.(Hons.) Counselling & Psychotherapy, Hypnotherapy, Reiki, CBT, NLP.

Please visit my website for further information or to schedule a private or corporate consultation.

https://susanmcelligott.com

INTRODUCTION

Everyone has a story, and the purpose of this book is to create a sense of hope. It aims to show you, the reader, how you can rewrite the script of your life no matter how old or deeply rooted your story has become.

Through storytelling, I aim to offer you some insight and hope, and the possibility of changing your disempowering thoughts which could be hijacking your happiness.

To enhance your experience, I have used an entertaining, light-hearted approach where appropriate. The purpose of this, is to show how positive change is possible, and can be faster than you think.

Each chapter explores an emotional challenge, and I have covered the same challenge in different stories, but from another person's perspective. This was intentional, to show how everyone has their own unique way of processing their thoughts, feelings, and beliefs. But one thing they all have in common, is the feeling of being 'stuck,' and wanting to change.

Throughout this book, you will find many useful and powerful 'mind mastery tools' including hypnotherapy, different forms of psychotherapy, neuro-linguistic-programming (NLP), energy psychology and cognitive behavioural therapy (CBT).

Some of the mind-altering psychological interventions are what I would refer to as 'unconventional,' and my style of facilitating change is not always what may be expected as the 'traditional' method of practicing therapy.

I have shared some of my own personal life experiences, along with real cases, drawn from over 20 years of clinical experience working in mental health.

I have included a bibliography for therapists or for those who would like to pursue further reading.

Maybe now is your time, to rethink and reboot?

THANKS FOR THE MEMORIES

Angela Mary Louise Hurton McElligott
You reared Winners!

AS PART of my life trajectory, I found myself becoming part of an end-of-life care team, which lasted several years. The life I am referring to is that of my own mother who had developed dementia in her early eighties and whose care lasted several years. This story aims to highlight the importance of focusing on what matters most in life when faced with end-of- life caregiving.

My family made the unanimous decision to support her in spending her final days in the comfort and security of her own home, where she had lived for over 60 years and raised her six children.

I was her eldest daughter, and this story is told from my own perspective. I have no doubt that my siblings could tell a different story, despite having the same purpose, in caring for our mother, we each had our own unique experiences.

Although they were challenging times, I learned a lot about interpersonal communication within family dynamics, along with the interactions of the many caregivers who were coming and going, to and from our family home. As my mother's dementia gradually progressed over the years, I became more aware of the meaning of end-of-life caregiving.

Although we all had the same intention, which was to give my mother the best possible care, and to make her as comfortable as possible during the final stages of her life, the variables in communication were diverse. Not only was there miscommunication between family members and professional caregivers, but there was also occasional disharmony within the family unit itself. For this reason, a timetable or roster was set up to include dates and times for the 24-hour care plan, and this was distributed to each family member. This allowed a smooth changeover while working alongside the professional caregivers.

THE TRAINED AND UNTRAINED

My grandfather had a saying which has remained in our family throughout the generations. And it goes like this: "There's a big difference between the 'trained' and the 'untrained' girl." So, as siblings, we often joked with each other in a competitive way to see who was performing the best! There was no special training, at least from my perspective, on how to manage a person with dementia. We just showed up as her adult children and did the best we could under unprecedented circumstances.

SUPPORT SYSTEMS IN PLACE

To communicate with each other, a logbook was placed on the kitchen table and before any interaction took place with my mother, the first thing that had to be done was to sign in and check for any instructions or recommendations on anything that needed attention. We would then log our opinions and interpretations on my mother's wellbeing for the next person's benefit. Since interpersonal, face to face communication was not always possible, this was the best way to convey information amongst the different caregivers. It was a way to keep track of everyone who was involved in my mother's care, and to pinpoint anything that might affect the quality of her caregiving.

This method appeared to work well on many levels as a means of communication between family members and professional caregivers. Its purpose was to ensure that my mother was receiving the best possible care. It was her 'voice,' a part of her, that dementia had taken away.

In her confused state, she had begun to get in and out of her bed repeatedly and needed constant vigilance, so we also installed a surveillance system to keep a close eye on her, for her own safety. We sought legal advice and followed protocol on how we could implement it, and everyone was aware of its presence. This meant, as a family, we could enjoy a certain degree of comfort and privacy, knowing that in the event her needing assistance during the night, we would be alerted immediately.

SLEEP DEPRIVED

One of the most difficult challenges I experienced as an overnight caregiver was the sleep deprivation. Despite the logbook and the surveillance system in place, it still didn't escape the fact that when I lay down at night, I would never be able to fully relax. In the latter part of her dementia, she was so confused, that her days turned into nights, and vice versa.

When I did manage to fall asleep, I was often woken up to the sound of her calling out, "hello, hello," It seemed to go on for hours. I never ignored those cries as it was too distressing for me to listen to, so I would have to force myself to wake up and gather my wits, to attend to whatever situation presented itself to me. Most of the time, it was a false alarm as she would not remember calling me at all. I would reassure her with some soothing words. Then, when she was settled, I would attempt to go back to sleep. This wasn't always easy since I was fully awake, and my mind was full of thoughts, about whether I had done the right thing or not. I needed something to help me sleep and I didn't want to succumb to taking medication, apart from the fact that I had to be responsible for my mother, who was in a vulnerable position.

PRACTICE WHAT YOU PREACH

A technique I often teach my clients is called, emotional freedom technique (EFT). This is a method of tapping on various energy points, or meridians, located around the body. It can be used for both physical and emotional pain, and it is often referred to as 'psychological acupressure.'

I personally found it to be extremely effective during this difficult time and in particular with my inability to sleep due to mental exhaustion. I was desperate and prepared to try anything and whenever I applied this technique, I would usually fall asleep within minutes. It never failed me, even during the most challenging times.

COMMUNICATION BREAKDOWN

The logbook saved my mother on more than one occasion, and the video surveillance system, in relation to the following incident, was invaluable.

One overnight stay was especially exhausting for me since I had been woken in the middle of the night by my mother calling out, "is there anyone there?" It was around 3am and I knew the drill. I checked the monitor by my bedside and could see that she was restless, and on the move. I forced myself to wake up and go swiftly downstairs and then try to appear alert and relaxed at the same time!

Despite her dementia, she was highly tuned into the energy of the people around her, and she could sense if someone was annoyed or anxious with her. I was tired and worn out, but when I opened her bedroom door, I made sure I had a smile on my face. She would always look surprised and happy to see me, and still had that child-like way about her. I offered her a choice to have breakfast, even though it was the middle of the night, she accepted with enthusiasm. Although I was tired, it was worth it to see the delight on her face and to hear her upbeat 'chatter' as she enjoyed her breakfast, her usual boiled egg and buttered toast. I could still communicate with her even when she struggled with some of her words, being a family member helped since I knew what she was trying to tell me. When she finished eating, I made sure she was comfortable and settled in bed before I went back to my own bed.

NIGHTMARE

What seemed like a few minutes of being asleep, I was suddenly woken by the sound of one of the caregivers shouting at my mother and calling her a 'blackguard!'

I got such a fright, and for a moment I thought I was dreaming, or should I say, having a nightmare. I immediately turned my attention to the monitor beside my bed. I could clearly see and hear everything. The caregiver was leaning over my mother as she was lying in bed, trying to force feed her. I saw my mother holding both arms against her face trying to block the food being forced upon her. I was horrified!

I instinctively, leapt out of bed, struggled to get down the stairs, still half asleep. In response to the commotion, I opened the bedroom door and stood behind the caregiver as she was leaning over my mother. I will never forget the look of fear on my mother's face as she struggled to protect herself. It was obvious that the caregiver was impatient and just wanted to do her job, presumably so she could 'tick all the boxes' for her employers.

I don't know how I composed myself when I told her my mother had already eaten breakfast at 3am and was obviously not hungry. The response I got was "how was I supposed to know?" to which I replied, "if you had checked the logbook, you would have seen that I had written a detailed report." She went silent at first, then tried to defend her actions by telling me about her own personal problems and how her head was, 'all over the place.'

I was very mindful of my mother's fragile state and didn't want to add further confusion and upset, so I quickly changed the subject as a means of distraction.

Once my mother was settled, I felt it was necessary to log the incident in the report book about the breakdown in communication, which had negatively impacted her. The inference that my mother was deliberately being difficult by using the term 'blackguard' to a woman with dementia, unable to communicate that she had already had breakfast and wasn't hungry, in my opinion was unacceptable. Only for the fact that I had been able to witness the incident myself, I shudder to think of what might have happened.

The outcome that followed was, that after a brief investigation, the 'professional' caregiver was dismissed from her post. I later learned that she directed the blame onto me for reporting it to her employers. But I knew I had made the right decision, to do what was right for my mother.

I CAN'T DO IT

I had found myself in unfamiliar territory and became blatantly aware of my limitations in my role as an end-of-life caregiver with no formal training or previous life-experience. It was a very uncertain and stressful period in my life. Occasionally, a 'professional caregiver' would encourage me to carry out a 'personal care' procedure for my mother, which was second nature to them, but for me, I found it impossible. I just could not do it no matter how much I tried, so I ended up feeling worthless and stressed out. If I were to be part of my mother's care-plan, then I would have to find a way to make myself useful.

I searched inside myself for any resources that I could use to get through this challenging time, and I soon found a way to do that. I connected to the part of me who was trained in my own professional skills in neuro linguistics (NLP).

This is a method of communication which offers insight into another person's inner world to discover how they process their own environment internally and externally. I had to find a way to communicate in the kind of language that I knew she would understand.

SOMEWHERE OVER THE RAINBOW

The 'art' of communication, when words may not be enough, can be a valuable tool when caring for a parent with dementia, and in my mother's case, her auditory senses were still finely tuned, and she lived for her music. She had a voice like a soprano and when she sang, her whole face would light up as she raised her head with pride, and that made her incredibly happy.

It would be fair to say that music was her life. She loved the arts and loved to perform recitations. One of her most sang pieces was by Judy Garland, 'Somewhere over the Rainbow' in 'The Wizard of Oz.' or a song from 'My Fair Lady,' 'I could have danced all night.'

She would often dress up by wearing hats and scarves to improvise another one of her favourite actors, Bette Davis, reciting a few one-liners from some of her favourite movies. She would often sing along with the actors as if she were playing the part herself! We all enjoyed her lively sense of humour and it would not be uncommon for her to burst into song at an impromptu moment.

LAUGHTER IS THE BEST MEDICINE

I came to realise that using humour was her way of coping with the many traumatic experiences, she endured throughout her own life. Grief and loss had darkened her door on many occasions over the years, and she often reminded me that if it wasn't for her love of music, she wouldn't have been able to get through those tough times. Music was her lifeline which would later become her legacy.

Since I grew up listening to classical music and her endless entertaining stories from her own childhood, I was comfortable and familiar with this way of communicating. Even though as a mental health professional, I would be trained to help people with many serious emotional challenges, this was different, this was my mother.

As I watched her slowly slipping away into a world of her own, I trusted my instincts. I knew we had a common interest in the performing arts, especially music, singing and poetry, so I would often sing one of her favourite songs. Despite having dementia, she never lost her love of singing and I would get an immediate response, as she often sang along with me. But unfortunately, as the disease progressed, the words of the songs and poems were gradually fading from her memory.

One experience I will never forget, during the earlier stages of her dementia, was a trip that was arranged for her to attend a day-care centre for senior citizens, in the hope she would enjoy some entertainment and social interaction. I could sense she was not too happy about the outing. Despite her laughs and play-acting, she was a very private person. She would not want the neighbours to think she needed minding. Before the minibus came to collect her from her home, she asked me if I would follow on and join her for a cup of tea, so I agreed. I stood by our garden wall to wave her off, and as the minibus drove off, she looked back at me with a slight wave of her hand. I had mixed feelings of sadness and joy. I suppose, for me, it was the stark realisation of the reality of an illness that was about to slowly invade her mind and I would eventually lose the mother who I had known to be quick witted and feisty. On the other hand, I felt a sense of relief for receiving support and a bit of temporary respite to be able to take care of myself and recharge. But at the same time, the guilt was always lurking in the back of my mind, am I doing enough?

When I arrived at the day-care centre, it was a strange experience to see her sitting in a circle amongst a group of elderly people, many of them in a semi-comatose state. They were waiting to be entertained by an elderly gentleman playing a piano in the corner of the room, and I was not prepared for what happened next, although, not surprised either. I noticed she had that mischievous smile on her face as she left her place in the circle of elderly attendees.

MAKING HER VOICE HEARD

She positioned herself next to the piano player and true to her character, raised her head proudly and began to sing! It was as if she went into an altered state and took on another persona or a character in a movie. Her voice was as powerful as ever, as she sang to her heart's content, regardless of whether her audience enjoyed it or not! The staff at the day-care centre gathered around to hear her sing and appeared to be highly impressed with her voice and her lively, fun personality. I still laugh when I reflect on that experience. It is one of those moments that will live on in my memory, and one I will always cherish.

THANKS FOR THE MEMORIES!

As the saying goes, 'life is what you make it' and it can never be as true as when you witness someone close to you living with dementia. Prior to her diagnosis, whenever I was leaving my mother's house, she would always escort me to the front door. Her parting words were always playful, and she would suddenly, without warning, start to improvise some famous actor. One of her favourite lines was a quote by the actor, Mae West, in the movie with Cary Grant, 'I'm No Angel.' as she mimicked the actress's tone of voice, "come up and see me sometime," and she would finish with, "and thanks for the memories".

As I tell the story of my mother and her light-hearted dramatic communicative style, it has become plain to see where I got my therapeutic style from, when working with my clients. As I recall and share my lived experiences, I realise more than ever, the importance of making memories.

MAKING MOVIES AND HOME ENTERTAINMENT

As my mother's memory was slowly fading, her long-term memory was becoming more to the forefront as she loved to reminisce about her past. This prompted me to gather some of her old photographs and compile them into a digital 'visionboard.' I added her favourite piece of music, from the musical, 'The King and I,' 'Getting to Know You.' We made our own movies, and she was the star of the show. Her reaction was priceless, as her whole face lit up, first with excitement, then with a lingering smile. I made many videos of her singing on her own and when she stumbled over the words, I would join in to help her out, so she wouldn't feel confused. Nevertheless, her favourite poem was 'Flow's Letter,' one we often recited together, and I wanted to learn the words so I could recite it to her.

One evening, as I sat at the bottom of her bed, reminiscing of 'times gone by.' While I was telling her some stories, I was going through and old suitcase containing some old black and white photos of hers which she loved to ponder over, when I came across an old poetry book belonging to her mother.

The book was covered in old torn wallpaper, and it was dated 1900's. As I opened it, there it was, on page 13, the infamous poem, 'Flow's Letter.'

And it goes like this...

> *A sweet little baby brother had come to live with Flo,*
> *and she wanted it brought to the table that it might eat and grow.*
> *'It must wait for a while' said Grandmama, in answer to her plea,*
> *'For a little thing that hasn't teeth can't eat like you and me'.*

*'Why hasn't it teeth, dear gran'ma?' asked Flo in
great surprise*
*'Oh my! But isn't it funny? No teeth! But nose and
eyes.*
*I guess the baby's toofies must have been forgot.
Can't we buy him some like grandpas? I'd like to know
why not.'*
*That afternoon, to the corner, with papers, pen, and ink,
Went Flo, saying 'Don't you talk - if you do, you'll
disturb my think.*
*I'm writing a letter gran'ma, to send to heaven tonight.
And 'cause it's very important, I want to get it right.'
At last, the letter was finished - a wonderful letter to see -*

*Directed up to heaven, and then Flo read it to me.
'Dear God, the baby you brought us was awfully nice
and sweet,
But because you forgot his toofies, the poor little thing
can't eat.'*
*'So that's why I'm writing this letter, on purpose to let
you know.
Please come and finish the baby - that's all, from little
Flo.'*

Written by Eben E Rexford (b 1848 d.1916) 'Everybody's Book of Recitations.'

THE PHOENIX BIRD RISES FROM THE ASHES

For as long as I can remember, the mythological figure of the 'Phoenix' bird represents how we can rise again. Out of the ashes of trauma, we can rise and soar above whatever challenges life brings us. Whether we immerse ourselves in the mindful act of listening to music to feed our souls, or whether we connect with the earth's energy, or nature's life-force through activities like walking in nature, gardening or preparing food, we can reconnect to our authentic selves.

I will be forever grateful for the many quotes and stories my mother told me throughout her life. They have ignited within me, a sense of wonder and curiosity which have kept them alive, to be retold and passed down through future generations.

Some of her favourite quotes were…

> *"Smile and the whole world smiles with you, weep and you weep alone."* ~ Jazlyn Roehl

> *"Nobody needs a smile so much as the one who has none to give.*
> *So, get used to smiling heart-warming smiles, and you will spread sunshine in a sometimes-dreary world."*
> *~ Lawrence G. Lovasik*

IT'S EITHER ME OR THE DOG!

The moment you change your perception, is the moment you change the chemistry in your body.
~ Bruce Lipton

THE FOLLOWING story describes how I treated one woman's forty-year dog phobia with a single session of hypnotherapy.

The story aims to show you how distorted thinking can have a profound effect on our lives. The power of the subconscious mind is evident within the narrative and depending on how you use that power, very much determines your outcome.

Maggie was forty-six years old when she came to see me for help with an intense fear of dogs. "I can't believe my husband and children could do this to me, after everything I have done for them, and this is how they treat me. They knew I had a phobia of dogs ever since I was a child, and they went ahead regardless and purchased a dog. We are all walking on eggshells and the tension and stress are unbearable. I don't feel safe in my own home and I'm a nervous wreck. I don't know what to do. Can you hypnotise me to overcome my fear of dogs?" Her voice trembled as she described how even the sight of a dog scared the living daylights out of her.

She stated that she was feeling under pressure from the people that were supposed to care about her, which left her feeling confused. Nevertheless, this fear had been the cause of immense misery for most of her life, for over forty years, and she wanted to get it sorted, one way or another. She admitted that she never had to seek professional help before. It was unfamiliar territory and completely out of her comfort zone but she was desperate.

I was curious to know what happened to her and asked her to tell me more. But Maggie laughed nervously, almost embarrassed to tell me the extent of her situation. She said she thought it was ridiculous that a grown woman could be acting so stupidly. She continued to laugh about it, but her bubbly, easy-going personality didn't hide her anxiety as much as she wanted it to. Her body was trembling and her voice stammered as she continued to make made small talk as if she were trying to hide her uneasiness.

OUT OF SIGHT, OUT OF MIND

Maggie's way of managing her phobia was to avoid looking at dogs altogether and pretend that they didn't exist. She was aware of the fact her children and husband had always wanted a dog, but there had never been a problem with it in the past. It was accepted, like an unwritten rule, that no dog could ever be around her due to her intense fear. Family life was good up until now, and she went on to tell me about the events which forced her to seek professional help to overcome her phobia.

From the moment she began to speak, her whole manner changed, and I could sense her light-hearted energy slowly draining from her, replaced by a look of sadness and despair.

She went on to say, "It all started about three months ago. I came home from work and there to greet me, was a small dog, just standing in the middle of my hallway." She said, "I will never forget the shock I got. I still remember the screams I let out. I was frozen with fear and unable to move. Suddenly, my husband came out of the kitchen when he heard me screaming. He quickly grabbed the dog and proceeded to try and convince me how cute and lovable he was. He did his best to persuade me to let him stay and I couldn't believe what I was hearing, especially when he knew I had such an intense fear of dogs. I told him that under no circumstances would I ever entertain the idea of owning a dog, ever, and that was my final decision. It was *not* up for discussion. I remember feeling a mixture of terror and rage all at once."

She had described her husband, Dave, as a kind, considerate man, so she was quite taken aback by this behaviour, which was completely out of character for him. She believed that after 20 years of marriage she knew him well, so she was not expecting this to happen. She said it felt like a form of betrayal to her. In addition to that, one of her two daughters, 18-year-old Jane, had lately become more confrontational towards her about the most minor things. This made her to wonder whether this whole affair had more of an effect on the family dynamics than she had realised, and it led her into a state of anxiety and confusion.

FROZEN IN FEAR

I asked her what happened to her that caused her to develop such a fear of dogs. She went on to explain about an incident that took place when she was about 6 years old, where she had 'allegedly' been attacked by a large dog. She remembered walking home from school, quite happy and carefree, when suddenly she noticed the dog sprawled across the entrance to his driveway. It was clear he was not tied up or restrained in any way. As she became aware of this, her mind went into overdrive imagining all sorts of scenarios that could happen if he were to come near her. Thoughts of how he could attack her were very real in her mind, and she remembered feeling a sharp pain in her stomach.

What followed confirmed her worst fears. She went on to tell me how the dog approached her from behind. She knew he was on her back as she could feel his heavy weight. She could feel the heat from his breath, as well as the sounds and sensations of his drooling and slobbering against the side of her face. She remembers feeling terrified and unable to move a muscle. Her body became rigid and immobilised for what seemed like an eternity.

It is often said that 'time is a great healer' but in this instance, it didn't apply. As she was relating the incident to me, her face was frowning and grimacing, her body was moving in a way that needed no words, to show that she was still suffering from the effects of that trauma, even after forty years.

FLIGHT WITH FRIGHT

During her ordeal, her friend, Emma, quickly intervened and somehow managed to distract the dog long enough for them to get away. She remembers her body reacting to the shock with trembling and shaking as she walked the short distance to her home. Her friend consoled her with encouraging words as she held her hand and did her best to lead her to a place of safety. Maggie had visions of being comforted by her father as soon as she got home. Instead, he took one look at her, rolled his eyes, called her 'a silly clown' and said, "that dog wouldn't touch you!"

Maggie's eyes filled up as she related her story to me, but she quickly wiped away her tears and let out a spontaneous release of laughter. She continued to giggle as she described how her fear of dogs was simply ridiculous at this stage of her life. Speaking it aloud caused her to feel ashamed and embarrassed, as she described herself as 'being silly.' She wondered why she had so many conflicting feelings, yet she continued to dismiss them. They made no sense to her at all.

She said she could never understand her husband's attraction to dogs. It was something she found impossible to imagine. Her probing looks in my direction, did not go unnoticed. Dismissing her fears as being 'silly' was not an option I would have chosen, I listened intently and then asked her to tell me more about herself.

Maggie pondered over the effects of her fear and the painful realisation of the destructive consequences they had on her relationships. She never thought she would find herself in such a difficult and vulnerable situation since she always considered herself to be strong and well able to handle most challenging situations in her life. For this reason, she didn't want to be portrayed as a victim. Despite this, she needed someone who would listen to her, and she didn't know what else to do or who to turn to, she was desperate for help.

THE TANGLED WEB OF FAMILY DYNAMICS

Family was always important to Maggie, it meant everything to her. She considered herself to be organised and kept everything in the home running smoothly. She was known as the 'go-to' person if someone needed a shoulder to cry on or a listening ear. She loved to laugh and have fun at every opportunity and always extended a warm welcome to anyone who came to her house. But this was no longer the case. She found herself having to deal with a different dynamic, a division within the family, since she was the only one who did not want the dog.

The introduction of the puppy into her home, in her view, was an unwelcome intrusion into her safe space since the only way she could avoid making eye contact with the Whippet was to hide away in her bedroom. For this reason, it was the only place in the house that she felt safe, and, unfortunately, she found herself becoming a prisoner in her own home.

Conflicting thoughts about her own guilt for not giving her family the choice to own a dog and whether she was being unfairly treated by them, began to take root. She became even more anxious and confused.

As time went on, she became increasingly detached from her usual routine, like cleaning the house or preparing home-cooked food. This was not corresponding with her core values as she always considered herself really house proud. She got a lot of satisfaction from taking care of the home. She loved to cook and enjoyed sitting at the table for family dinners where everyone shared their daily happenings.

However, during the past three months, since the family brought the dog home, the atmosphere in the home had now become noticeably tense and awkward. For instance, when she walked into a room, she noticed her husband 'played down' his enthusiasm and his love for the dog by making sudden gestures of disinterest but it was so obvious and made her feel uncomfortable. Her daughters behaved in similar ways, so as not to upset her, everyone was walking on eggshells.

The stress was also taking its toll on her marriage which she always considered to be rock solid. She found herself on shaky ground, feeling completely overwhelmed with a combination of different emotions including fear, frustration, anger, and hopelessness. The irony of this was, that her husband provided a sanctuary or safe place for animals when he was growing up. Now she was the one who needed a place of safety. Her once cheerful home was now in danger of falling apart and she feared that things may never be the same again. Something had to be done or she could lose everything she loved and worked so hard to build over the years.

HYPNOSIS LEADS THE WAY

Since Maggie had already begun to relax her body. I began the hypnotic process by guiding her with positive suggestions that she would soon experience a deep state of relaxation, allowing a gradual release of any tension she was holding in her body.

My intention was to bypass the 'critical factor,' in other words, the conscious logic brain that tries to make sense of our experiences. This generally reduces any possible resistance to change. I observed her willingness to place her trust in me, as someone who could help her overcome her fear. She was finally ready to face the truth.

Exploring her lived experiences, meant going deeper into the hidden, repressed parts of her subconscious mind where the roots of her fears were buried.

It was obvious when Maggie told her story that she was suffering from a condition known as Post Traumatic Stress Disorder, (PTSD). She showed all the symptoms of someone who was trapped in a 'trancelike state' as she was attempting to describe her phobia. I encouraged her to notice what was going on inside her mind during the hypnotic process and to share whatever thoughts emerged.

I knew she loved to use humour to cover up her anxiety. She naturally made light of her problem using casual, dismissive remarks about herself. This strategy appeared to work for her on a surface level, but it was not enough to reduce the overwhelming fear that she had endured for over forty years. Nevertheless, I encouraged her 'humorous part' to hang around during the hypnotic trance, and when the time was right for her, we would use it in the appropriate context, to help lift her fear.

One of my greatest mentors was Roy Hunter who introduced me to this useful and powerful technique, 'Parts Work.' The concept is simple but effective. The idea is to explore certain traits or characteristics of someone's personality with the intention of negotiating with them for positive solutions in a non-confrontational way. I have successfully used this method, combined with hypnosis, for over twenty years, and it continues to get some amazing results.

MEETING HER YOUNGER SELF

It takes courage and trust to journey into the deeper parts of the mind, but Maggie's fear was so great that it was a decision that she welcomed, if it meant releasing her fear. She knew at a deeper level, what she had to do to be free from old unwanted programming and unhelpful beliefs. I acted as her guide, but she was the one who had the answers to her problem. The time had come to deal with 'unfinished business' in her past.

Using hypnosis and Gestalt psychotherapy to unravel her beliefs, she was able to discover what she thought was impossible, until now. I guided her to travel back in time to meet her younger self at age 6 as she was walking home from her 'girl guides' club with her friend Emma. As she connected with her 'child part,' she was able to recall exact details of the 'incident' with the dog.

ROOT CAUSE

As she began to recall the details, it was not long before her body responded to the changes taking place at a visceral level, since she began to flinch and twist in the chair. Her facial expressions became more dramatic in intensity as she remembered feeling the weight of the dogs' paws on her back and experiencing a 'tugging' sensation, as he tried to pull the tassel off her hat.

She could describe the smell and sensation of his warm breath and the wet dribble on the side of her face as if she was feeling it all over again. She recalled being terrified, as her body responded by becoming rigid and immobile. It seemed to go on for an eternity and she said she thought she was going to die.

Suddenly, her eight-year-old friend Emma, came to her rescue and managed to save her by chasing the dog away. The next thing she remembered was being comforted by her friend and almost immediately feeling a sense of relief, when she no longer felt the weight of the dog on her back. She remembered the sound of Emma's reassuring words which were so comforting to her, and all she wanted to do was go home and feel safe. There was nothing else to report about the 'alleged' attack.

At his point in the session, while Maggie was still in a hypnotic trance, I could tell by her facial expressions, that she was experiencing an epiphany or an awakening, as if she was realising for the first time in forty years, that she had not been attacked in the way she had originally thought! She discovered, to her amazement, that the dog was merely being curious and playful. However, the trauma didn't end there.

When she was escorted home, she wasn't prepared for the response she received. She imagined a scenario of being comforted by her parents, but this didn't happen. Her father, who, incidentally, she described as a good man, and who she always enjoyed a close relationship with, told her she was being silly, and that the dog wouldn't touch her.

Within the mind of a six-year-old child, the message she received from her father was that her feelings were not important. It didn't matter to her what his intentions were since she didn't feel safe and secure. All she heard was, I must be stupid to have this fear, and even worse, was the embarrassment of her friend Emma who had witnessed it. She wondered what her friend must have thought about her and her family.

The feelings of being dismissed were too painful to handle as a young child. They became repressed in her subconscious mind, where time is irrelevant, waiting to be triggered, and ignited, forty years later.

Maggie only wanted her father to protect her and to reassure her everything was going to be ok. She began to wonder if he was right. What if she was, like he said, just a 'big clown?' Despite her belief about how stupid she was to think such ridiculous thoughts, she could not help feeling embarrassed and ashamed as well. She remembered, as a young girl, feeling dismissed, rejected and alone, as if she was not worthy or good enough.

Another memory surfaced while she was in trance. It was of her siblings laughing at her. They thought it was hilarious what happened to her and they sided with their father when he called her a 'silly clown' for being afraid of the neighbour's dog. Everyone knew, except her of course, that the dog was harmless. She didn't expect the response she got and she continued to wonder what her friend must have thought about her family.

While Maggie was recalling these past traumatic events, I encouraged her to be more aware of how her body was responding to those emotions now. She recoiled her body in the chair with dramatic squirming and twisting movements.

She was clearly struggling even to put into words how she was feeling, but eventually, she uttered the words," he's like a 'bag of germs,' he's disgusting!" She described the dog as 'skittish.' I challenged her, humorously, to define what she meant by 'skittish,' as I had never heard the word before and wasn't familiar with it. She burst out laughing as she tried to describe to me what she meant, and she rephrased the word, using something similar, as she described the dog as being like a 'jittery ball of fur,' when he makes sudden movements as soon as he sees her.

It appeared that the bare glimpse of the dog's presence was enough to stimulate a negative reaction in her. There wasn't even time to 'rationalise' what just happened, it was an automatic response, of an earth-shattering scream. Her behaviour not only frightened herself, but also the dog who was forced to run for cover. She realised, at that moment, that she was behaving exactly like her dog. She was unconsciously mirroring the dogs' mannerisms, by being, in her own words...... a bit 'jittery'!

NEW CHALLENGES

If Maggie wanted to get back to living a normal life, she knew she would have to face some new tough challenges. She would have to muster up a lot of courage within herself. She knew she was courageous from earlier experiences but was not sure how to use it in a way that could help her with her dog phobia.

Using a playful approach, I asked her which one was the most 'jittery,' was it her or the dog? She responded with an outburst of laughter. It was as if she suddenly realised, with new awareness, how ridiculous it sounded, now that she was able to say it aloud, and hear her own voice echoing back to her.

I was curious to learn more about the dog and asked her what breed it was so I could get an idea of what he looked like. She muttered quietly that it was a white-coloured Whippet named Cian. Her fear was so debilitating that she never had the courage to look directly at him.

With her permission, I searched the internet for images of the breed she was referring to, so I could get an idea of what he looked like. She nervously confirmed it matched the image of her dog and she still managed to laugh. I encouraged Maggie to look at her situation differently, to help her 'construct' a new scenario in her mind which was more aligned with her own needs, and in particular her strong family values.

In this case, I asked her if she could begin to consider how the dog must be feeling and if she could imagine it from his perspective. I remarked that the poor dog didn't choose his owners or what kind of home he was forced to live in. Her response was one of immediate surprise and laughter.

A DOG'S LIFE

I have encountered many challenges in my career as a hypnotherapist in finding the right approach for my clients, but I have never previously had to improvise a dog! Nevertheless, I embraced the challenge to explore life from the dog's perspective. I wondered what a little Whippet puppy would sound like if he had a voice and could speak. What would he have to say about his living conditions?

I proceeded to change the tone of my voice and speak for the dog like this: "here I am just wanting to be loved and cared for... instead what do I get?!! ... this screaming, hysterical woman who is terrifying the life out of me with all her crazy 'jittery' movements...what did I ever do to deserve this stressful situation? ...why couldn't I have been brought into a 'normal' kind family who would appreciate my lovability? ...I have a beautifully soft, non-shedding coat which is so sleek and velvety soft to touch and no nasty doggy smell off me ….and I'm extremely low upkeep… the occasional trip to the groomers isn't much to ask to keep me looking so lovely now, is it? The husband likes me, and her two lovely daughters think I'm just the best thing that ever came inside the door of this house…. why can't she be like them and accept me into what I thought was this lovely kind, caring family?"

Maggie couldn't contain herself as she burst out laughing at my exaggerated, dramatical description of her dog's predicament. I wasn't sure if it was the sound of my voice pretending to be the dog, but whatever made her laugh, it was working. I could see her whole energy change to become more relaxed and happier. Whatever shifted in her caused her to connect to a part within herself that allowed her to feel empathy for the dog.

Through hypnosis, we were able to explore her ability to switch places with the dog and get an opportunity to see it from his perspective. I knew Maggie was a kind, caring and devoted mother, so I used this quality in her as a strength or resource to help her. I continued with my 'doggy' voice to say, "I am terrified of this woman who keeps screaming at me….no wonder I get 'jittery' and 'skittish' …would you blame me? What else am I supposed to do when she shakes her body in that scary way…. look at the size of me…. I'm so small and vulnerable."

I was aware of her memory of being that small vulnerable child who was once scared herself, and I wanted her to have the opportunity to heal herself by experiencing that same vulnerability again. But this time it would be different since she now had all the necessary skills to help herself. She was able to find and use her inner strengths as a caring, nurturing mother with her lived experience as a forty-six-year-old mature woman capable of thinking differently and applying it to herself directly.

LOSING THE FEAR

Just at that moment, a look of sadness appeared on her face as she let out a deep sigh and her body sank back into the chair. As she was relating her story, it was as if she suddenly realised something she hadn't thought of before now.

Her facial expression changed again but it wasn't anger on this occasion, it was more of a deflated look as she admitted to feelings of guilt and shame. She felt it was her fault for denying her children important and valuable experiences while they were growing up and she began to feel sorry for them. She referred to her fear of dogs as her 'baggage' from her own past and her husband and children were having to pay the price.

She went on to describe how her husband grew up surrounded by dogs of all types as his family ran a rescue shelter. It was then he developed a natural love of animals. The thought crossed her mind that this new puppy he brought home was his way of recreating the same enjoyment that he had experienced as a child. She paused for a moment, then added, "What if it were the case that all he wanted was for his children to be able to enjoy the same experience?"

I interjected with, what if the learnings from this distress produced a way of understanding that what other people experience often has nothing to do with us, and could often be a projection of our own pain?

It did not take long for that 'shift' to occur because, just then, I noticed Maggie's voice began to change. Her tone became much softer as she connected to her more mature, motherly part. The realisation that she had something enormously powerful within herself that she could now use to help herself, was becoming a reality. It was there all along, but she had not made that connection, until now. Tears followed as Maggie broke down sobbing, but she was crying for the little girl, her six-year-old self who felt emotionally abandoned by her father. The same feelings revisited her in her adult life as her husband behaved similarly.

She realised now that it was a distorted belief she had somehow embraced and if she were to be honest with herself, none of it was true. Both her father and her husband loved her and did not intend to hurt her. Once she accepted this new belief, she was free to let go of the old one that they didn't care about her. This time, her tears reflected a sense of relief and gratitude within her.

NEW LIFE NEW PATH

In follow up sessions, we did a further, more holistic exploration of the quality of her relationships overall. She was now able to look at her life through many different lenses knowing she was responsible for her own thoughts and was free to choose how to 'respond' rather than 'react' to any situation.

She found to her surprise, that the energy the dog had brought into her home was very peaceful and relaxing. She said, all he wanted to do was curl up beside her at every opportunity, and she went as far as saying he was such a 'friendly and lovable dog.'

She admitted that the dog had inadvertently taught her some new skills. Personal communication had improved as she developed new ways of looking at things. She found she had much more understanding, patience, and empathy, especially with herself.

Her husband was delighted and so proud of her willingness to overcome her fear. Her self-confidence grew every day as she ventured out for walks with her puppy. Friends and co-workers were surprised, even though they knew her to be a light-hearted person anyway, but this level of confidence was something they hadn't seen before. She was finally 'de-hypnotised' and free to enjoy her life in ways she had never thought possible.

The feelings of strength and resilience were now becoming a part of her as she finally began to appreciate a newfound sense of freedom. It was a strange but liberating experience for Maggie to realise that she could now look forward to getting her life back on track and bring a sense of normality back into her home life.

The outcome of this collaborative approach to change, meant that we are not alone in this world. It is through our connectedness that we learn the most about ourselves. It takes courage to face our deepest fears, which often keeps us stuck. And, it is often through suffering, that we find our greatest opportunities to grow, and become better version of ourselves.

Sometimes, we must have a 'breakdown' before we have a 'breakthrough.'

"Dogs do speak, but only to those who know how to listen."– Orhan Pamuk

NOT DOGS AGAIN!

"Our deepest fear is that we are powerful beyond measure. It is our light, not our darkness, that most frightens us. We ask ourselves, who am I to be brilliant, gorgeous, talented, fabulous?" ~ Nelson Mandela

SWEET REWARDS

THIS INTERESTING AND delightful little story relates to a pair of young six-year-old twin siblings, Jenny, and Simon, who developed an enormous fear of dogs, for the 'sweetest' of reasons.

It all started at an outdoor family birthday party. While everyone was enjoying a fun time, a jeep drove into the farmyard. It was the children's uncle Paul arriving with more party balloons and treats. Without a second thought, he opened the tailgate of the jeep to let out his two Labrador dogs, who bounced out and landed near where the twins were playing. The dogs began sniffing around, just enough to satisfy their curiosity, and then lay down on the grass to stretch themselves after their journey.

The uncle assured everyone his dogs were very friendly and there was nothing to worry about. The twins didn't seem to agree since their screams could be heard by everyone at the party, as they ran indoors. Unfortunately, no amount of reassurance could convince the children that it was safe to come outside again, and they had to leave the party at once.

Since that incident, the children have never been able to return to their uncle's house for fear of seeing the dogs again. The effects on the children were devastating, and to this day, even the sight of a dog, no matter what size, would send them into a state of sheer panic. The result was that the parents were unable to visit their extended family, which included many of the cousins, so everyone was losing out on family gatherings. Anne's brother, who owned the dogs was not forthcoming with any solutions, as he felt his dogs were not a threat. According to him, they were the most well-behaved, gentle dogs you could meet.

Anne, the children's mother, was at her wit's end, as she felt everyone in the family was paying the price. Family get-togethers had now become a major problem for them. Since they didn't want a repeat performance of what happened at her brother's house, they felt it would not be fair to expect the children to endure any further trauma.

THE SWEETEST GRANNY

The experience turned into an even bigger problem at Granny's house, who looked after them while their parents were at work. She too, was 'caught up' in the drama. Playing outdoors was a nightmare as there were dogs everywhere and it didn't matter whether they were restrained or not. Their fear of being attacked by a dog was so overwhelming, it usually resulted in outbursts of hysteria, causing the twins to run for their lives.

Granny wanted to help and did her best to try and comfort them. She always had a supply of chocolates and sweet treats for special occasions. And she felt that this was indeed one of those occasions. She thought, what could be more important than when her grandchildren needed comforting?

Her ploy appeared to be working, at least temporarily, because as soon as the children came running indoors after seeing any kind of dog, they would immediately calm down and relax, when they were offered the treats. Unfortunately, it didn't solve the problem, and their fear of dogs continued.

In this situation, I agreed to treat the children in their own home environment. I decided to bring along my canine assistant, my old faithful dog, Timmy. When I arrived at their home, I received a warm welcome from parents, John, and Anne, who appeared to be reserved and shy. As I was being offered a cup of tea, I couldn't help noticing a large amount of chocolate biscuits and treats on the table. I was told they were put there in the event of the children becoming distressed, while I was helping them to overcome their fear. I didn't say anything but knew they wouldn't be part of my approach.

BUILDING TRUST

At this point, Jenny and Simon were hiding under the kitchen table and when summoned to greet me, they nervously crawled along the floor, and then clung to their mother's side.

If I were to succeed in gaining their trust, I had to think quickly as I might only get one chance to succeed in building rapport with these frightened children. I turned my head away from them and looked out the kitchen window and I noticed they had a trampoline in their back garden. I fixed my attention on it to create a distraction, and I told them how much I loved trampolines, and asked whether it would be ok for me to try it out.

At this point, I was beginning to question my own sanity, but my focus was on helping the children with their phobia. I was prepared to do anything to restore some form of normality within the family. I could see the look of shock and surprise on Jenny's face, but curiosity got the better of her as she peeked out from hiding behind her mother. She grabbed her brother's arm, and they bolted past me towards the garden, and jumped onto the trampoline themselves. I presumed it was their way of saying "this is our trampoline," which was exactly what I had hoped would happen. The twins were taking the lead, and I was willing to follow them.

SETTING THE STAGE

I managed to climb onto the trampoline, with some difficulty, and began to jump up and down with the children, much to their delight. Any nervous tension they showed earlier had disappeared, so I challenged them to jump higher than me. It didn't take much persuasion for them to try and outsmart me. I suggested we play a pretend game, so I asked them if they could be any animal, which one would they choose to be. I began by saying "I want to be an eagle, and I'm going to spread my wings far and wide as I glide through the sky watching everyone below me becoming smaller."

Without hesitation, the children started to improvise various animal movements, and were really getting into the dramatics. Then, I invited them to enter my 'Animal Kingdom,' but first, they would have to pass a test, by making various animal sounds. This would mean they would need to prove how brave they were. I could tell by the look on their faces that their imagination was activated, as their voices changed and adapted to making sounds of different kinds of animals. They started to roar and screech and growl and howl. They were so excited to act out the animal game and to qualify for the 'fearless warrior' award, that awaited them when they could carry out the final task ...to stroke the head or tail of my dog, Timmy.

A WISE OLD DOG

Their ears perked up as they listened carefully to my story about Timmy. I explained to them that he had travelled a long distance and was now very tired, so he was relaxing in the back seat of my car. The children listened intently about Timmy about how he loved traveling with me with his collection of stuffed toys. Everyone loved his relaxed, laid-back energy. The children's eyes glazed over as if they were trying to recreate that image in their minds. They wanted to learn more about Timmy. But there was something important they needed to know. He was an old and gentle animal. His sight and hearing were not good, so he needed to be shown lots of patience. He especially loved children who knew how to be kind to him and only very gently stroking his head and tail and he always enjoyed the attention.

THE ANIMAL KINGDOM

But first, they needed to use the superpowers of their own minds to be able to gain access to the make-believe 'animal brain' inside their own heads. They would need to do this to gain permission to enter the 'Animal Kingdom' if they were to succeed in their mission to stroke Timmy's head or tail. They could choose one or both, it was up to them. If they could do both, it meant achieving even greater superpowers.

> Note: At this point, I am creating what is called the 'bridge effect' to create a smooth transition from a stressful event to a place of safety in the mind of the sufferer. The 'trigger'

may still be experienced, but this time, a safe bridge or gap is created, allowing room for a new response. The 'safe place' is created within their own minds, which is the 'superpower' that they were able to connect with, using the imaginary 'animal kingdom.' This helps to develop a process of self-regulation, by changing the association attached to their fear, and substitute it for a newer, more positive meaning.

OUT OF THE MOUTHS OF BABES

At last, Jenny and Simon agreed to stroke Timmy, and they appeared ready and willing to do the challenge. I was so happy for them, that they finally agreed to break through their fears to go meet Timmy. In preparation for this, I asked them to imagine how amazing they are going to feel, when they tell their parents that they stroked Timmy. Just then, six-year-old Jenny reached over and whispered into her brother's ear "We will tell them in two weeks." I was flabbergasted, to say the least, I did not expect to hear that!

SECONDARY GAINS

I soon realised that the fear of dogs was more than what it seemed on the surface. There was an obvious hidden agenda that served them on another level. I thought it was time to bring the grownups into the picture.

When it was revealed how the children had come up with a plan to not tell their parents of their bravery, both parents were flabbergasted at their shrewdness, but could not help laughing at the same time. It became clear that the children had more than a vested interest in continuing with their 'fears.' The more they acted scared, the more they would get rewarded with treats, hugs and kisses, and words of comfort. A plan of action was needed to teach the children healthier coping skills to self-regulate when needed.

THE GROWNUPS WORLD

While the children were learning how to overcome their fear of dogs, an interesting disclosure emerged, which made an important contribution to the outcome of the sessions.

John, the children's father, admitted, that for most of his life he was disguising a dread of dogs. He thought he was doing well at hiding it from his children, but now his children appeared to be copying him, as they too had developed the same intense fear of dogs that he was 'hiding.'

> Note: There is some evidence that fears run in families so that the person who is afraid of animals is more likely to have a parent who displays similar fears. For example, parents sometimes instil fears of dogs in children by repeatedly warning their child of the dangers of big dogs. This results in generating a self-perpetuating cycle of avoidance and fear. 'Avoidance behaviour' is a basic way to down-regulate hyper-arousal, and is often used as a backup strategy, if there is no control of the situation. This strategy was what the children had learned.

FACING THE FEAR

It was time to introduce my sixteen-year-old dog, Timmy, to the family. Most people were drawn to my dog as he radiated an inner wisdom and calmness.

It is hard to describe in words, but when he moved, he did it elegantly, with a humble bow of his head. His non-threatening movements showed a friendliness that earned him many pats on his head and gentle strokes on his back. He would respond with a calm acceptance as he twitched his nostrils using his 'animal intuition' to sense the human spirit. And when he was satisfied with the 'assessment,' he would wander off in a meandering, carefree fashion. We can learn a lot from animals and Timmy was, in my biased opinion, the best teacher on how to communicate non-verbally. He had successfully managed to gain the family's trust as they all gravitated towards him, to give him lots of hugs and praise.

To help build the children's self-confidence, I offered them some dog treats, and suggested they could reward Timmy for his good behaviour. Jenny smiled nervously and looked at Simon, who clearly wanted to do it. Their nervousness was overcome by enthusiasm, as they grabbed the treats. Granny began praising them for being so brave and their parents agreed that it was a major step forward for the children.

THERAPEUTIC CHAMELEON

While working with young children, I often find myself just like a chameleon, always changing and adapting to the needs of the individual and always exploring to find what works best for them. In this case, where they are either too young or too traumatised to ask for help themselves, then a direct approach is not much good, or can even be counterproductive. Humans come with all different personalities and temperaments, so do animals. It's all about mutual trust and respect. A person who has not learned emotional regulation does not have a way to differentiate between rational and irrational fears. So, spending some time in the presence of a harmless animal, develops and strengthens feelings of safety and self-assurance. You must learn to control your fear, and do not allow it to be the cause of missing the pleasure of knowing and understanding animals.

TEACHING AN OLD DOG NEW TRICKS

After this breakthrough, John felt inspired by his children's bravery, and wondered whether it was possible to overcome his own fear. He had come to realise how much it was impacting not only himself, but his entire family. He agreed that life would be a lot easier if he could learn to handle his own triggers and reactions to dogs. He eventually agreed to face his own fears, which, thankfully, did not involve trampolines! In his case, it was again, a learned behaviour, which needed to be unscrambled and restructured in his mind, using hypnosis (age appropriate), and other psychotherapeutic interventions. Nevertheless, the outcome yielded positive results.

End Note:

> The amygdala, a primitive part of the brain, which is responsible for the 'flight or fright' response, cannot figure out what to do about the change. The executive, decision-making part of the brain, takes care of that. Learning to recognise signs of safety, like when a dog is on a leash, builds confidence and ends avoidance behaviours. Breaking the challenge into small steps, by linking each step to a positive emotion, has been known to be effective. This is usually a *visual* and *auditory* stimulus that helps develop more realistic, alternative ways of thinking. By *expecting* to feel fearful, during exposure practices, and *realising* that what is happening is not as *catastrophic* as one might expect, is a highly effective way to lessen the fear. This is often enough to be able to function normally.
>
> In cases of post-traumatic stress disorder (PTSD), painful emotions can be stored in the body and often need some form of therapeutic intervention to release them.
>
> Trauma can cause the body to become rigid with fear, so any kind of **physical movement**, which accounts for 55% of

communication, can be the perfect way to allow this to happen naturally.

The **tone** of our voices and how we **sound,** accounts for 38% of communication. So, it's not *what* you say but *how* you say it, that counts for the way we choose to express ourselves.

The **words** or *content* used, account for only 7%,

And most importantly, laughter can never be underestimated as a therapeutic tool or intervention, for the purpose of releasing trauma or stored emotions.

TAKING THE BISCUIT

*Everyone needs a sense of shame,
but no one needs to feel ashamed.*
—*Frederick Nietzsche*

JACOB WAS A STURDY, obese 45-year-old man with a warm smile and easy-going disposition. He was full of banter and chit-chat and my initial impressions were that he was super confident. The banter and smiles continued as he described his predicament.

He told me that he had recently noticed how unfit and tired he had become, and his clothes no longer fit properly. He had developed an addiction to chocolate biscuits and wanted to get his weight under control. Despite wanting to lose weight as a self-confessed chocoholic, he had a very unusual compulsion that was bothering him, and despite his joking remarks, he appeared a bit awkward or embarrassed as he began explaining it to me.

DISAPPEARING BISCUITS

He admitted that he had a compulsion to sneak into his sister's house via the backdoor and steal biscuits from her biscuit tin. He had obtained a spare key and knew she had kept them in a cupboard, hidden away from her kids. Grinning from ear to ear and highly amused.

He explained how this behaviour provided great entertainment for him since it created a huge mystery amongst his entire family as to how the biscuits were disappearing. He went on to say that his younger sister, Marietta, was baffled as she couldn't figure out how the biscuits were vanishing. She would leave her house for work early in the morning and by the time she returned in the evening, half the biscuit tin would be empty. She was beginning to doubt herself and even questioned her sanity.

He continued laughing as he related the story, and the highlight of his thrills was for him to know the truth when no one else did. He had succeeded in 'outsmarting' them all and had them all baffled and confused.

I began to wonder what it was all about, then; my curiosity was short-lived as his expression changed. He stopped joking around and he took on a more serious demeanour, lowering his head, he slumped back into the chair and clenched his hands together as if he needed to soothe himself with what he was about to divulge.

What was once exciting and thrilling to him, had turned into feelings of embarrassment, shame, and guilt and his compulsion to steal biscuits from his sister's house was causing him to feel overwhelmed.

He told me that he could not understand why he felt compelled to carry on with this silly, unnecessary behaviour and the planning and scheming were taking over his life and it was consuming his every thought. He had developed a highly intrusive obsessive-compulsive thinking pattern which affected his ability to concentrate at work and he was becoming anxious and worried he might lose his job because of it, he felt powerless.

He couldn't understand why he was acting this way, he considered himself to be accomplished man of means, so there was no reason for him to steal biscuits. It has gotten completely out of hand; what started out as a joke had backfired, now the joke was on him, and he did not know how to stop it, he called it, "a living nightmare."

HIS STORY

I was curious to find out more about Jacob and asked him what life was like for him as child. He described it as mostly positive with many happy memories of life growing up on a farm with his parents and younger sister, Marietta.

He remembered that his mother was always baking, and he still recalls the smell of home cooking coming from the kitchen and it was a comforting experience that the whole family enjoyed. Jacob recalled how his mother even baked her own biscuits and it was something he grew up with and never questioned it, it was all he had ever known.

Then, he found it strange and became curious as to why his mother would go out and buy biscuits from a shop whenever she had visitors. He laughed as he was telling me, that it would be considered a privilege today if you were served home-made biscuits.

I could tell by that remark that Jacob was trying to rationalise events from his past, but when we explored further, we found out that there was much more to his story than he had even realised. His mind created his own interpretation of events and no amount of talking it through was going to solve the mystery of the compulsion to steal his sisters' biscuits.

When the 'conscious will' and the 'subconscious imagination' are in conflict, there is no contest, the imagination wins every time, without exception. ~ Emile Coue

My task now was to steer him in a direction that would involve a much deeper dive into that part of his mind where the answers were buried, to join the dots and see the bigger picture of what the driving force behind his actions was. What was he gaining from this unusual behaviour? Stealing the biscuits was one thing, but the way he went about doing it was something that needed further exploration if we were to get to the truth.

I listened to Jacob's story intently as he reminisced on his childhood memories. He related how he loved to play tricks on everyone at home and he gloated freely at how he succeeded in confusing them.

He went on to say how he pretended he had done his homework after school and would wait until the whole family had gone to sleep, then he would sneak downstairs and do it by candlelight. He would then creep back upstairs like a thief in the night and climb into his bed, sometimes at 3 or 4am. He was exhausted, but the positive feelings he got from performing this activity far outweighed the negative. He seemed quite pleased with himself as he was smirking and boasting, to the point of being arrogant, about his nocturnal adventures and how he had outsmarted them all.

THE HYPNOTIC TRANCE

To access the emotional brain, it was necessary to bypass what is known as the 'conscious critical faculty' our internal filter.

This is the part of our brain that we use to logically interpret our own unique lived experiences. We try to cognitively make sense of our experiences and link and connect similarities between present and past experiences. *Unfortunately, this is like opening up the attic door when you want to go down into the basement to find what you're looking for.*

As he was relating his story, Jacob was clearly in a heightened state of anxiety and excitement as his eyes glazed over and I could tell he had spontaneously entered a hypnotic trance. I utilised his 'altered' state and guided him by direct suggestions to release any tension that he may be holding in his body. He responded by leaving out a long 'sigh' as he became physically and emotionally still and calm.

I invited him to take his mind back to a time in his former, younger, developing years and to allow any memories to surface without using any conscious force. I did not want him to use any logic or reasoning at this point.

He began by telling me that when he was around 7 years old, he remembered his mother was setting the table using her best china tea service. Although he was quite young, he was aware that they must be for special people, since his mother was making a huge effort to have everything exactly right. He remembers been told to play quietly in another room, with his sister, Marietta, and to stay out of the way. She also told them not to touch the fancy shop bought biscuits as they were for the visitors, but they were allowed to have one of her home-made biscuits instead.

Jacob felt an overwhelming curiosity about the 'forbidden' room and what all the fuss was about. He was intrigued, so while his mother was occupied elsewhere, he couldn't help himself, he remembered tiptoeing along the hallway and opening the door to the living room, his heart pounding with the fear of being caught but he somehow found the courage to go inside and look at the 'forbidden' biscuits on display.

CAUGHT IN THE ACT

It was like a daring adventure in the scene of a movie, and he was the leading actor. He felt a mixture of fear and excitement and couldn't believe his eyes when he saw the spread of fancy chocolate delicacies. He began to salivate at the thought of tasting one and when the temptation overcame him, his fear soon disappeared, as he reached out to grab one. He remembers savouring every morsel of the forbidden biscuit as it melted in his mouth. It was like nothing he ever imagined; he was in heaven.

Just at that moment, his sister followed him into the room, and as soon as she saw him eating the chocolate biscuit, she screamed aloud. "*Oh, my God......I'm telling mother on you!*"

Jacob went on to say, "I will never forget the drama that followed, and my short-lived indulgence soon came to a grinding halt. I was now going to be exposed as Marietta blew the whistle on me. How could she betray me like that? I would never do that to her, I hate her now!"

I can still hear my mother's voice echoing in the hallway as she called out my name, *JACOB!* I was terrified. She made me stand next to the plate of chocolate biscuits and although it was obvious there was a couple missing from the plate, she still asked the question in a sharp, angry tone of voice …. "*didn't I tell you not to touch those biscuits? You knew they were only meant for the visitors?*"

"I will never forget the look on her face. She was furious with me. Any positive feelings of adventure and thrill seeking had vanished, and I was left feeling humiliated and disgraced. I made a complete fool of myself! What made matters worse was her sister, my aunt, was standing behind her and witnessed everything. My sister looked so self-righteous and smug, I wanted to wipe that look off her face."

Since Jacob was in a deep hypnotic state, the emotions began to surface from his subconscious mind in the form of images of his past. He continued to describe the effects of the 'forbidden' chocolate biscuits that were meant for the 'visitors.

He recalled the short-lived moment of pleasure he got from the taste of chocolate melting in his mouth, it was nothing like he had ever imagined in his life, and he wanted to recreate that wonderful experience.

SECRET PROMISES

He made a promise to himself that when he grew up and could afford to buy his own chocolate, he would indulge himself with unlimited supplies without the fear of being deprived. He was determined to re-experience that feeling of 'being in heaven' as he remembered it.

His dreams came true when he successfully landed himself an office job where he could secretly hide his stash of chocolate in his desk drawers, and no one would know.

He carefully drew up a plan where he could purchase chocolate without being recognised. He would drive great distances to different petrol stations where he would appear as a new customer, without fear of being judged.

He smiled as he told me had it down to a fine art. Meanwhile, his weight began to creep up with the amount of junk food he was consuming and that was something he was unable to hide.

It was obvious that Jacob had undeniably gained a sense of power and satisfaction from 'getting the better of' or 'outsmarting' his sister by cunningly entering her house and secretly raiding her biscuit tin.

WHAT YOU RESIST PERSISTS

So, I felt it would be useful to use a 'paradoxical' approach to increase his sense of power and control and to encourage those feelings, for now. I knew the way the subconscious mind operates in this respect and had I not gone along with him; the danger is that it would have created unconscious resistance. It would be met by a 'cul-de-sac' or a dead end for sure. If I had gone against him with shame and guilt, it would drive his anxiety or neurosis even deeper. So, I encouraged Jacob to indulge his fantasy of getting the 'upper-hand' or 'outsmarting' others, and in particular his sister. In his mind, he was in control now and *nobody* was going to dispute it. According to him, he had won.

UNRAVELLING THE MYSTERY

As Jacob's story unfolded, it became clearer that there were many connections and similarities between his present obsessive, compulsive habit, and past events. In his words, he was humiliated by his mother and betrayed by his sister, and he, subconsciously, needed to find a way to settle the score in his mind.

In his pursuit for revenge on his sister Marietta, Jacob was beginning to realise how his behaviour was affecting others. He had not considered how his habit could impact her children, his nieces, and nephews. His sister had bought those biscuits for her children, and he was stealing them. She had hidden them up high in a cupboard but had every intention of sharing them with her family.

He admitted that she was not saving them for any 'special visitors,' and had always been exceedingly kind and generous when he came to visit her home. She always welcomed him since he was her only sibling. She had, most likely, forgotten all about that incident when they were younger. After all, telling tales on your brother when you are only 5 years old is a natural part of growing up. He just wanted to teach her a lesson, but his sister had no idea he felt this way about her, even if it was driven by a subconscious desire for revenge.

Jacob then realised that the only person he was hurting was himself as his sister had no idea why or how her biscuits were disappearing. In his quest for control and self-empowerment, he found himself in the grips of a prison of his own making. He felt trapped and betrayed within his own world of deception and trickery.

'Holding a grudge is like eating poison and expecting the other person to die' ~ Buddha

FREEDOM AT LAST

Tears flowed down Jacob's cheeks as he finally realised how much he had sabotaged his own freedom and happiness in his desire to seek revenge and justice for his younger self. His perception of not being 'good enough' to have the store-bought chocolate biscuits, sent him on a path of deception, manipulation and lies. His mission now was to set himself free from his 'victim mentality' created by his own sense of betrayal by his sister.

Journeying into the deepest part of his subconscious mind, Jacob was able to travel through time and reconnect with the 'part' of him that suffered feelings of shame, embarrassment, and humiliation. He had the opportunity to connect with his inner child who was not allowed to touch the forbidden biscuits. They were only for special people, so, in his mind, that meant that his mother must have thought he was not 'good enough.'

He began to reflect on the part of him that was daring and adventurous at such an early age. He saw that it was the only way he knew how to cope when he was a young boy. He began to recognise that, as he was growing up, those qualities got him through many challenging life situations. By changing his perception on those aspects of his character, and channeling them in a positive direction, Jacob was able to appreciate himself more. He was able to forgive the part of him that sought justice in such a misguided way. He never meant to cause harm to anybody and when he communicated this awareness to his 'child' part, he noticed a 'shift' in his energy.

He felt like a whole weight had lifted off his shoulders and felt ready to release the excess weight his body was carrying. He realised that it was not about the chocolate after all or anything he was eating, it was more about what was eating him. He realised that he was an intelligent, creative person with an enthusiastic sense of fun and adventure. These were the qualities that everyone loved about him and the belief that he was not good enough, was an old, outdated 'thought pattern' from his past due to a 'cognitive error' or a 'distorted belief.'

Jacob's compulsion could be seen as negative and destructive, but there was a positive, secondary gain.... he would never have to face his fears or have to deal with the painful emotions that overwhelmed him. Instead, he repressed them, but they eventually found their way to the surface, in the form of obsessive-compulsive disorder (OCD).
The anger and humiliation that he felt as a child, manifested as stuck energy in his body and since he did not know how to change it, he developed a fixation on secretly stealing biscuits from his sister in the hope of releasing that energy.

Universal law: 'Energy cannot be created or destroyed, it can only be transformed from one form to another.'

In Jacob's case, the energy transformed from anger and humiliation to cunning, scheming and deviousness. The time had come to let go and release all the pain and hurt that no longer served him. He was willing to forgive, not only those who unwittingly caused him suffering but himself for not knowing any better....

And, when we know better, we do better ~ *Maya Angelou*

BONJOUR KARMA

"What doesn't kill you, makes you stronger."
~ Friedrick Nietzsche

MY INTEREST in foreign languages could easily be described as my hobby or pastime. While most of my peers would be listening to the latest pop music, I would be glued to the foreign radio stations, hoping to perfect my pronunciation, and I never went anywhere without a French dictionary to hand.

Because of my keen interest in the French language, I was aware of being treated favourably by my French teacher, Miss Donegan, or so I thought.

During the summer, before my final year at school, at the age of sixteen, I had an opportunity to travel to Spain to work as an au-pair. I didn't have one word of Spanish except 'si' and 'no.' I was not at all familiar with the language, but my role was to speak only in English to a family of six children, ranging in age between 2 – 12 years. It was an experience of a lifetime as they were part of the Spanish royal family, Count, and Countess.

During my stay, I hadn't heard any English spoken and so by the end of my 4-month term in Spain, I returned home to Ireland, speaking fluently, like a native Spaniard. I was so excited with my new language skills that I decided to sit my school's final year exam in this subject. But since Spanish was not part of the curriculum, I required special permission to be allowed to do it, which I was given. I arranged private tuition to perfect the written grammar so I could sit the exam and everything seemed to be going well for me.

KILLJOY

I continued studying Spanish along with lessons in French, Irish, Latin and English. It was hard work, but I loved it.

I was happy doing 'my own thing' until my French teacher, Miss Donegan, made it clear to me she was not impressed. She couldn't hide her disappointment in me when she learned about my trip to Spain. I could tell she was testing me during French class, when she called out my name, "Susan McElligott, what were you doing in Spain?" "Speaking French, were you?" to which I replied, "yes Miss." I will never forget the look of indignation on her face and her harsh tone of voice. I knew she was furious with me. I had to think of something to say so I said, "well, my French helped me converse with people who didn't speak English." But my reply didn't satisfy her, and I could sense she was disgusted with me as I was always the pupil she would go to when she asked a question in French. She would often ask me to speak in the correct tone or pronunciation to demonstrate to the class, during a lesson, but not this time. When she asked me to translate a sentence, I 'sang' it to her, with an obvious Spanish tone. She went silent, like she was lost for words, and it was then that I knew, I was no longer her favourite pupil.

One day I will never forget, was when one of the teachers did not show up for class and the students became loud and boisterous. I remember not wanting to have anything to do with the chaos in the classroom. I tried my best to get on with my studies for my next class, which happened to be French. The sound of footsteps on the school corridor instantly turned to silence, it was Miss Donegan, and she was not happy. It would not be an exaggeration to say she was raging as she glared around the classroom looking for any obvious signs of blame, but she was met with complete silence. She was determined to find out who was responsible and when no one owned up, she directed her gaze towards me. I could feel her anger and frustration. What happened next, created a defining moment in my life, and had a devastating effect on my self-confidence.

UNREASONABLE EXPECTATIONS

When she did not get a response from anyone in the class, she said, "Susan McElligott, tell me, who is responsible for this?" I replied truthfully, "sorry Miss, I was reading my French book and didn't see anything." When she didn't get the response that she expected from me, which in effect was to 'snitch' on my classmates, her eyes narrowed, and her voice became stern. I will always remember the look of disgust on her face as she uttered the words, "Oh, never mind, you were always a problem pupil anyway."

That statement she made when I was sixteen years of age, in the presence of my peers, caused me to feel like I had done something wrong. It plagued me for years and became one of my life's most defining moments.

THE STUDENT IS READY, AND THE TEACHER APPEARS

Fast-forward forty years and while holidaying in Spain with my husband, at a lovely hotel, right on the beachfront. The sun was setting, and I was wearing sunglasses, but I couldn't mistake 'that walk.' I couldn't believe my eyes. I thought, no, it couldn't be, yes, it was... Miss Donegan! My eyes followed her as she walked along the promenade, a short distance from where I was sitting. She had that same 'walk' with her head held high, wearing a wide brimmed sunhat and a long silk scarf that trailed after her in the breeze. Her husband walked a few paces behind her, as she led the way.

I was guessing that she must have been in her late 70's or early 80's by now, but she had that way about her like she always did, that hadn't changed, even though it was forty years later.

I was instantly triggered when I saw her, and all those feelings I felt when I was sixteen years of age, instantly came flooding back. I recoiled in my seat and gripped my husband's arm as I pointed her out to him. He had no idea what was happening to me as I tried to hide behind him so she wouldn't recognise me. I told him not to make eye contact or focus any attention in her direction.

I set off to my hotel room to attend to an online call and left my husband to relax until I got back. When I finished my call, I was taken by surprise when he 'innocently' called me over to a table outside by the pool. I was looking forward to enjoying the evening to unwind, when he said he wanted to introduce me to some people he had met earlier. He told me they were keen to meet his wife and wanted to know what type of work she was doing in the hotel room. He guided me towards the table where the infamous Miss Donegan was seated with her husband. To say I was caught off guard, was an understatement

EMOTIONAL TRIGGERS

I cannot describe the overwhelming surge of emotions that erupted inside me at that moment. I approached her table as a nervous, innocent, studious sixteen-year-old, afraid to say the wrong thing in case I would upset her. But then, something strange happened. It was like I was floating above myself as I was seeing events playing out in front of me. I felt like I was an observer, and not really there at all. She beckoned me to come join her and her husband for after dinner drinks by the pool. Her voice had the same high-pitched tone as she asked me to tell her more about my work.

Suddenly, I was aware of being guided by a wisdom far greater than myself. I was no longer communicating with Miss Donegan as her pupil, I was now able to relate to her as her equal. But beneath my confident demeanour, I couldn't help wondering whether she was going to delve into my past and discover who I really was.

THE PHOENIX BIRD RISES

The tremendous fear and dread of being exposed as her once 'troublesome' pupil was inescapable. But as I began to speak, I could feel a burning surge of energy rising from the depths of my being, and I was no longer the shy, nervous sixteen-year-old girl, crippled with fear. I was now a professional woman in my late 50's, a wife, mother, and grandmother who had overcome many of life's challenges, and had not only survived but thrived.

KARMA REVISITED

Then, the conversation took an unexpected turn when she told me that her daughter was having some problems with her sixteen-year-old daughter, her granddaughter, and wondered if I would be willing to help. She told me that the family tried everything to get her to conform to house rules, but she was out of control, and they were at their wits end. She was practically begging me at this stage, and I could hardly believe what I was hearing, if only she knew who I was. She never recognised me at all. I thought about it for a moment and decided to put aside any emotions I may still have been harbouring about her. If I were to practice what I preached to my clients, I had to forgive her for any wrongdoing towards me. I knew I had to let go of any need in me, to judge her or to expect her to be any different. My purpose or trajectory in life was to help others, so my decision to help her granddaughter, was perfectly aligned with my own core values.

LESSON LEARNED

Soon after, I had the opportunity to help Miss Donegan's granddaughter, and to be honest, it gave me a sense of closure from any emotional wounds which were inflicted on me by her grandmother. She will never know, not even to this day, how much her comments affected me by how much they had impacted my self-confidence. Yet, it had become one of the 'defining' moments in my life, for it was through this experience, along with similar distressing setbacks, that led me down this path of helping others to overcome similar experiences.

The entire experience from start to finish, was a lesson that no classroom could ever teach me. There were no language skills capable of interpreting the magnitude of the learnings I was able to apply to my life and to my work.

It is for this reason; I see forgiveness as a gift to myself as I choose to use the experiences of my past as the building blocks for my continued perseverance and resilience

It was only through life's challenges I learned my greatest lessons which have transformed to become some of my greatest strengths.

'No one can make you feel inferior, without your consent.' ~ *Eleanor Roosevelt*

SHADOWS OF DOUBT

You are the master of your destiny.
You can influence, direct, and control your own environment.
You can make your life what you want it to be.
~ Napoleon Hill

I FELT it important to include this chapter in the book since I want to bring awareness about something that often lurks in the shadows of the innocent and the vulnerable.

I am talking about 'Gaslighting,' a term used to describe a subtle form of control and manipulation and can lead to feelings of anxiety, despair, helplessness, and depression.

If you've ever felt like your thoughts and feelings were being ignored and disregarded, and you start to question yourself whether it could be all your fault, then you may be gaslighted.

It is when you are being told repeatedly that what you think or feel, isn't true, even though you know deep down, it clearly is. Or if you find yourself listening to so called 'factual' information without evidence to back it up, and then being pressured into believing that it is true. Or, if someone denies saying something, even when you clearly heard it. When this happens often enough, the victim starts to question themselves and their sanity, which only makes the abuser more powerful in the relationship.

In the movie Gaslight (1944), a man manipulates his wife to the point where she thinks she is losing her mind. Gaslighting is a form of emotional abuse that's not always obvious and can be difficult to spot. They begin to make subtle remarks that can leave you questioning yourself and wondering if you really heard it or you were overreacting at what was being said. But no matter how small these comments may seem, they are still harmful because they make people doubt themselves and their perceptions of reality, which, on its own, can be really damaging.

You may not want to tell anyone in case they think you are being irrational or overly dramatic, so you feel trapped inside your head and the thoughts are going round and round, in a continuous loop, and this is when it gets confusing. You begin to feel ashamed, so you often become isolated from friends and family as you don't want to burden them with all this absurdity.

REVELATION

Awareness is key, and it is the first step to protecting yourself from this covert, manipulative form of control.

Identifying the signs, feelings of overwhelm, panic, helplessness, depression are all normal reactions to abnormal circumstances and realising that you are not going mad or overreacting.

Do not expect sympathy or understanding from them as they often lack the ability to see your viewpoint. They usually act charmingly and may tell you what they think you want to hear, to mislead you into thinking they really care about your needs. Gaslighters are good at manipulating those they perceive as being vulnerable or weak and they take advantage of that.

PLAYING GAMES

Do not play the game with them or be fooled into believing it is love, if you feel hurt and you are suffering, it isn't love. Other people's actions that negatively impact us, are usually a reflection of their own inner world and that is not something you ever want to get curious about. There is no amount of energy spent trying to 'fix' someone else's behaviour, worth sacrificing your own peace and happiness. Everyone is responsible for themselves.

OUR INNER CRITIC

When you have been a victim of gaslighting, unless you have learned the tools of how to escape from the trap, it can follow you around like a deceitful shadow. It can take on a life of its own within your own mind and be extremely hard to shake off. It then becomes a form of 'internal gaslighting.'

You have become your own worst enemy, but this time, you are the perpetrator, because you are doing it to yourself. You will know if this has occurred when the signs start to appear. Some definitive examples are:

When you begin to doubt your own worthiness and dismiss your feelings as unimportant.

When you believe that others will think you are stupid or not good enough, if you have to speak in front of a crowd.

When you feel embarrassed by compliments and praise from others to the point of dismissing yourself or putting yourself down.

When you give up on yourself and don't bother trying, in case you might fail, despite the fact that others can see your good points, but you can't, or you fear they might think you are being conceited or boastful.

You deserve better than to put up with being gaslighted inside your own mind. Be compassionate with yourself, and do not mistake your vulnerability or your kind nature as a sign of weakness or stupidity.

PINK ELEPHANT

'Energy flows where your attention goes,' so, when you tell yourself not to think of something, your brain must first create the image of the very thing you don't want to think about. Try not to think of a pink elephant and see what happens. Whatever you focus on, will expand, so when you develop a more positive 'growth mindset' you will gravitate towards a more confident version of yourself.

When you choose courage and take action, you are free to let go of the suffering. Pain is inevitable, suffering is optional.

Imagine, if you could open your mind to the possibility of inventing an imaginary friend that is assigned to supervise and filter all your thoughts, what would that feel like?

The decision is in yours. When are you ready for the change to begin now?

Control your own destiny, or someone else will ~ Jack Welch

SILENT ANGER

"Anger is nothing more than an outward expression of hurt, fear and frustration." - Phillip C. McGraw

Graham was a good-looking young man in his early 30's, and judging by his physical appearance, he liked to work out and keep in shape. But he had a dark, sinister look, and for a moment, I was caught off-guard.

As I looked at him, he produced a blank stare that looked right through me, and I was curious to learn what was hiding behind that dark veil of mystery. I wondered what had caused him to put up this barrier, and if he was willing to work with me towards breaking through the wall, he had built around himself.

His passive indifference became a way of coping, in order to mask his anger. It appeared he had already given up hope of resolving whatever was going on for him, since his friend had to persuade him to seek my help.

The look of apathy and despair that surrounded him needed no words. I was curious to learn what life circumstances reduced him to this helpless state.

I introduced myself in my usual chatty manner with the intention of making him feel safe, without judgement, so he would have an opportunity to be heard and understood. I was mindful of my choice of words and rather than asking him what his problem was, or what was 'wrong' with him, I asked him "what happened to you?"

He lowered his head and shuffled to compose himself. He proceeded to offer me chapter and verse of his life, involving constant hospital visits and doctors' appointments. He listed several medical terms and labels that were put on him over the years and had begun to normalise this way of living. The various medicines that doctors had prescribed for him, had not brought much relief. Any hope of feeling normal again, gradually faded away.

Graham went on to tell me that he had a problem with controlling his anger. He remembered being bullied for much of his childhood. He was not very tall and was always self-conscious about his physical appearance and others noticed his vulnerability and began teasing and taunting him to get a reaction. He would always rise to the bait and felt an overwhelming urge to defend himself.

When he got triggered, it was like a rollercoaster that he could not get off once the wheels of rage were set in motion. He described the onset of emotions that began as a mild irritation, which then led to frustration, before escalating into a full-blown outburst of anger and rage. This was the opposite outcome to what he had wanted. He desperately needed to feel in control, but he just could not do it. Instead, he felt powerless as the anger had escalated to a point of no return.

As soon as the rage subsided, he felt disgusted with himself for losing his temper. When he would strike out in anger, they would laugh at him and tease him even more. There was no end to the torture he endured.

He remembered feeling isolated, and he had no one to stand up for him. Social skills and tolerating stress were challenging to him, he became obsessed with how he looked physically so he developed an eating disorder. He devised his own program which involved strict regimes and self-imposed challenges for gaining physical strength.

The pressure got too much for him and eventually it led to periods of long-term therapy with psychologists and psychiatrists. He told me how one of the psychologists misinterpreted his words and reported back to his parents a completely different picture that did not reflect what was really going on for him. This resulted in a breakdown of communication with the therapist and a loss of trust which hindered any further progress.

His feelings of being ignored triggered something in him that was later to contribute to his mental health problems. He was then given a diagnosis of borderline personality disorder (BPD), which explained his extremely sensitive nature and his tendency to being easily triggered. His feelings of being dismissed followed him into his workplace and caused him even further problems. He considered himself to be good at problem-solving with difficult work-related tasks but again, it often went unnoticed.

Despite being dedicated to his job, he felt he was not getting the recognition he deserved. This would cause him to get frustrated, go into a rage and start slamming things around or raising his voice on the phone to his colleagues. He said it gave him a temporary release of frustration, but he knew deep down, it was causing him even more anguish and pain. He had to find another way of handling his emotions.

BURNING RAGE

Graham described his anger like a burning sensation in the pit of his stomach, and before he knew it, he experienced a piercing headache that started at the base of his skull and made its way to the front of his head and out through his eye sockets. He said it was excruciating. At this point, all logic reasoning had disappeared and there was nothing he could do to stop the explosion of anger that was going on inside his head. Nothing else mattered, except wanting revenge. He HAD to do something…anything—to create a feeling, that gave him a sense of power and importance, without any regard for the consequences.

He had an overwhelming urge to feel physical pain and to feel the force of adrenaline rushing through his body. He used his fists to punch walls until he felt the satisfaction of seeing the blood dripping from his knuckles… to know he had the power to stand up for himself and feel important. But the aftermath only left him feeling ashamed and even more hopeless as he lost complete control of his senses. The 'high' from all these pent-up emotions, resulted in severe insomnia. He was unable to sleep for days and had reached a point of not caring anymore.

A LIVING NIGHTMARE

Desperation drove him to taking sleeping tablets to get relief from his racing thoughts, but his mind would not switch off from the constant chatter of his own voice saying, "what's the point? no one listens to me anyway; I just want to sleep and for the noise in my head to stop."

The next thing Graham was aware of, was waking up in a hospital psychiatric ward three days later with multiple stab wounds all over his body and he had no idea of how he got there. This form of self-harm is often related to what's known as 'the silent scream.' It meant he could no longer handle his painful internal emotions. He would intentionally cut himself to externalise his feelings, as the level of anguish or distress were unimaginable. At this point, the physical consequences were not considered a priority. He needed to feel relief no matter what.

> Note:
>
> Healing is more about discovery than recovery since we are constantly being faced with life's challenges. Often the people who trigger us to feel negative emotions can be viewed as messengers for the unhealed parts of us.
>
> Dr. Gabor Mate refers to the term, 'Compassionate enquiry,' and is about holding a space to allow the traumatised person to feel safe enough to explore their beliefs and where they came from; and guide them towards letting go of the hold that their stories have on them.

HEALING THE TRIGGERED PART

Finding a way to break the cycle of his dysfunctional thought patterns and lifelong behaviour habits, was a necessary part of the healing process. We needed to recognise his triggers and why they were causing him so much pain. Graham's need to be heard did not go unnoticed as he went on to tell me what 'happened' to him in harrowing detail.

I wanted him to actively take part in his own healing journey. So, together, we named his triggers and engaged in brainstorming sessions to find ways to manage his anger, frustrations, and feelings of being dismissed and unheard.

Recognising he had choices on how to respond to any given situation was a game changer for Graham. It never occurred to him that he had the freedom to choose whether to react or respond, when faced with unwanted thoughts or behaviours.

In this instance, I offered him a strategy in neuro-linguistic programming (NLP), called a 'pattern interrupt,' which allows him to create that safe space between stimulus and response. Graham found this really useful in helping him to gain control of his racing thoughts and learn to hijack them before they had a chance to take root.

The practice of keeping a journal and watching his thoughts helped to keep him on track, make him accountable and expand his confidence and self-belief.

LABELS

Graham had lived with labels for as long as he could remember, and he thought they were useful at the time since it meant that whatever was 'wrong' with him, was real. It meant someone understood, yet his life was still in chaos. Instead of getting better, those 'labels' were reinforcing his problems, causing him to remain stuck and become detached from life altogether.

His family support was good and he had a very close relationship with both parents who were always willing to listen to him. And his sister was always there for him.

Unfortunately, for Graham, it wasn't enough, he needed to gain the respect from his peers, and to feel he mattered. He was not backing down, whatever price he had to pay.

FINDING A NEW IDENTITY

Graham had formed a unique, new-found identity as a result of a collaborative approach in building his self-awareness. At the end of his final session, he revealed several tattoos on his chest of spiritual symbols, with specific meanings, relating to his own beliefs. He was smiling proudly as he showed them to me. It was his way of saying; "this is me and I am a unique human being, and I have no desire to conform to the opinions of others!"

He said he no longer felt the need to defend himself in anger. He had finally found peace inside a spiritual home within himself.

Holding on to anger is like grasping a hot coal with the intent of throwing it at someone else; you are the one who gets burned. ~ *Buddha*

BURDENS OF SHAME

*"When we are no longer able to change a situation,
we are challenged to change ourselves."*
*"Everything can be taken from a man but one thing:
the last of the human freedoms — to choose one's attitude in any
given set of circumstances, to choose one's own way."*
~Viktor Frankl

JOHN WAS A TALL, smartly dressed gentleman in his mid 60's who captivated my attention with his charming quick-witted sense of humour. I could have been fooled into believing he didn't have a care in the world but there was something about him that was not so obvious.

Despite his smiles and light-hearted banter, his eyes could not lie, and I began to wonder how I could help him. It is often said that the eyes are the 'windows of the soul,' and I was intrigued to learn more. I explained that we would be working in a collaborative manner to achieve the best possible outcome for him.

As a design engineer, John appeared to be open minded and felt he could relate well to this approach, and he proceeded to give me a brief background of his life. He told me he was happily married for over thirty years and how he was blessed with four children and six grandchildren, who he referred to as 'the light of his life.'

He had recently retired from the business world which rewarded him with financial success. He appeared to have the perfect life, but it was obvious there was something bothering him. He hesitated for a moment while he tried to gather his thoughts, and then, it was as if he was suddenly lost for words. He shuffled nervously for a few moments as he lowered his eyes, cleared his throat, and muttered the words, "I feel stuck, and I can't explain why."

Considering that words only account for 7% of communication, I encouraged him to find another way to express himself. He immediately placed his hand on his stomach and looked at me for reassurance. I leaned towards him and nodded to let him know that I understood what he was saying, without any need for words. The most important thing was that he was able to communicate in a way that he felt heard and understood.

John's medical history revealed he had undergone many medical tests over the years to try and figure out a cause for his stomach pain, but nothing showed up physically. He was later diagnosed with a psychological condition of post traumatic disorder or PTSD, which suggested it was probably 'all in his head.' He was then prescribed anti-depressants and anti-anxiety medications to help lift his mood and sleeping pills to help switch off from his internal chatter. He did improve for a brief period but no matter how much he tried to push away the unwanted thoughts and feelings, the stronger they became. Wherever he went, they followed him. He had lost the ability to feel any joy or happiness in anything, not even his grandchildren. He was desperate, and willing to try anything to get some form of relief. He thought there had to be more to life than living like this, so he pushed it to the back of his mind, refused to look back and decided to focus all his energy on his work.

He was determined to create a better life for his family and give them the security and comforts he never had. At the same time, he looked forward to retiring one day and enjoying quality time with them, and especially his grandchildren. But, when the time came to do just that, instead of feeling joy and happiness, he became like an observer, detached and withdrawn. He began to fake feeling good, like it was something he was 'supposed' to do, but he knew he was living a lie. John admitted to spending a lot of time over the years in and out of psychiatric hospitals for occasional bouts of severe depression.

To try and help himself, he began reading self-help books and learning psychology. But no matter how hard he tried; he could not get past those dark feelings that had been plaguing him no matter what he did or where he went. He was exhausted from the constant battle to find peace and the thoughts of never experiencing happiness scared him.

NIGHTMARE REALITY

I was curious to learn more about his past. He told me he remembered being a happy child up to the age of five and then his life took a turn for the worst and the unimaginable happened.

His mother gave birth to his baby brother, Jim. He remembers being curious about the new arrival and wasn't sure what to expect or how he would feel about it. But when his father arrived home with the baby, there was no sign of his mother. When he asked where she was and when she was coming home, he said he will never forget the look on his father's face as he told him that his mother was never coming home. She had developed complications during the birth and died, but the baby had survived. After the initial shock, he remembered what can only be described as a burning rage welling up inside him towards his baby brother. As far as he was concerned, he was responsible for destroying his life. He recalled standing over his brother's crib uttering the words, "I HATE YOU!"

Tragically, a short time later, his father had also passed on; it was a living nightmare. He discovered several years later, the truth of what really happened to his father. He did try to take care of him and his new-born baby brother, but it all became too much for him to bear, and he took his own life. This left the children orphaned. In those days, it wasn't possible to find a foster home that would take care of both siblings together, so they became separated for many years and only reunited when they were well into their adulthood.

John said that he will never forget the feelings of bewilderment and abandonment the day he taken away from his home. He had vivid recollections of being ushered into the back seat of a car and driven for what seemed like hours and hours, to be placed in foster care. He felt his world had fallen apart, everything that was familiar to him, was suddenly gone.

His experience in the foster home was not a happy one as there were many other foster children living under the one roof. He could never understand why his brother was not able to come with him and why they could not be together. There were many unanswered questions, and no one seemed to care or take the time to explain anything to him.

He remembers feeling lost and lonely without his parents and brother. The once safe and secure life which was familiar to him was now gone and he didn't know when he would ever feel secure or happy again. That feeling of despair and sadness stayed with him throughout his life, for as long as he could remember.

HOUSE OF HORRORS

When he was about twelve or thirteen years old, he became rebellious and troublesome, so he was placed in an Irish Catholic industrial institution for children. It was there that he suffered the most shocking brutality and traumatic abuse at the hands of the clergy, the people who were supposed to be looking after him. He was subjected to forced labour and he was at the mercy of clerical pedophiles.

The abuse continued until his mid-teens as he continued to live in fear and dread of not conforming to the 'rules.' He soon learned new ways to survive including detachment from his emotions to block out the pain. These resources which served him well during those challenging times but paradoxically were to become part of his greatest obstacles.

FREEDOM AT LAST

John said that he will never forget the feeling of freedom and relief the day he walked out of the grounds of that building and he could hardly believe he was free at last. But that feeling was short-lived. Although the abuse he had suffered had ended, his mind was still processing the trauma, trying to make sense of it when there wasn't any. He became plagued with recurring nightmares which played over and over in his head, which often left him completely exhausted. The more he tried to forget or resist the images of what happened to him, the more intrusive and persistent they became. He eventually learned to live with it and accept that it was part of his life's trajectory. He had given up all hope of recovery.

His brain had not caught up with his successes in having achieved so much despite the awful hardship he endured. He felt he had every reason to be happy or at least, content in his life now, but the shadow of his past just would not go away and leave him in peace.

SIBLINGS REUNITE

When John was released from the Catholic institution, an uncle arranged temporary accommodation and employment for him on his farm. This gave him a start, until he could figure out what he wanted to do with his life. His uncle was a man of few words and was not the type to get involved in anyone's business. He supplied practical help to John as a gesture of goodwill, being a blood relative. John's experience in the institution was never spoken about and he just 'got on with it' and was only glad to be free.

Sometime after, he began to wonder if it were possible to find his younger brother Jim and to find out if he was all right. So, after some enquiries in various sectors, he eventually tracked him down in another town only a few hours away from their parent's home. Jim had the good fortune to have been placed within a loving family environment and he seemed quite happy with his life. He did not have any memories of their mother or father as he was much too young at the time to recall when they were both taken away from their home.

Although John was excited to meet his brother, it was a bittersweet moment for him. He was happy to see him but at the same time, he felt sad. He thought about the missed opportunities of growing up together and wondered what life would have been like if they had been able to bond as brothers despite the five-year age gap.

He wondered whether he would have turned out differently had he not endured the horrendous abuse at the hands of the Catholic clergy. Despite his happiness at being reunited with his brother, he could not help feeling a certain resentment creeping in since his brother didn't suffer like he did. The feeling made him feel uncomfortable, but he was unable to control it. Since Jim was his only sibling, he wanted to feel excited and happy to be reunited after all the years of being apart. But the more he tried to ignore the resentment, the more it intensified, and he became ashamed of feeling so mean-spirited. Then the guilt set in, as he dug a deeper hole for himself and didn't know how to get out. His mind would not shut off a constant flow of repetitive, negative, intrusive thoughts.

STRUGGLING IN THE ABYSS

In the years that followed, John was determined to make a difference in the world by helping others who were victims of abuse. Driven by the traumatic experiences he had endured in the institution, he set up a charitable organisation for children who came from broken homes. He worked alongside his brother who was already working in the area of mental health, and it appeared to be a success. John thought that this venture would make him feel valued and fulfilled, but it was not enough, it only reminded him of his own pain and unhealed parts of himself.

He began to reflect more on his own life and realised that he had never been given an opportunity to mourn the loss of his parents. No one had ever even mentioned it to him. It was as if they never existed. He continued to be haunted by the ghosts of his past and the unrelenting anger about the abuse he suffered at the hands of his 'guardians.' John described himself as feeling trapped inside a deep dark hole and could not see a way out.

IMPRISONED BY THOUGHTS

His life was once again in turmoil and at one level, he knew he was no longer a helpless child. He was a competent, confident adult who was now free to make his own choices. He tried to distract himself with doing courses in further education and he began researching any information that might help him. He recited daily mantras to flood his mind with optimistic thoughts, avoided any form of reflecting on his past, as he wanted to 'move on' and think positively.

By then, his body was responding to the stress and pressure of trying to manage his emotional state. All the hospital tests were carried out and the results showed that there was nothing physically wrong with him. The doctors could do no more for him. He was then transferred to a psychiatric unit since the only conclusion they could arrive at, was that it was most probably 'all in his head.' He could not bring himself to reveal the awful truth of what happened to him in the Catholic institution because the shame of it was just too much for him to bear. The more he tried to avoid thinking about the events of his past, the more it followed him around and eventually, it caught up with him.

EARTH ANGEL

During the several months stay at the psychiatric hospital, his brother, Jim, came to visit him every day and showed a great deal of concern for his wellbeing. He was so helpful, kind, and caring, there was nothing he would not do for him to get better. Jim's training as a social worker were invaluable in contributing to a speedy recovery and John was so grateful for his support.

Meanwhile, Jim was unaware of his brothers' resentful feelings towards him, and that made John feel even more ashamed and guilty. Even though Jim was skilled in mental health training, John still could not bring himself to admit to the thoughts that were plaguing his mind. His brother did not deserve to hear it, especially after everything they went through, and he could not see any benefit in revealing his true feelings. It was enough that his brother invested time and effort in supporting him through his mental breakdown, then to expect him to endure a further burden of a secret resentment towards him. He could never reveal to him how he blamed him for being responsible for losing their mother after giving him life. Yet he could not let go of his secret anger.

HOPE IS NEAR.

John's story was filled with many complexities. However, it's often been said, *'where there's life, there's hope'* and the fact he continued to search for help was a positive sign, it meant he had not given up entirely.

I wanted to find the path of least resistance since I was mindful of the burden John was continuing to carry. So, being a grandparent myself, I was able to connect with him with a mutual level of understanding. I encouraged him to talk about more about his grandchildren and it didn't take long for his face to light up when he spoke about them. I could see how much they meant to him when he smiled quietly to himself, and at the same time, his eyes filled with tears. He confessed that it was one of the main reasons he wanted help, since he noticed his grandchildren beginning to sense his unhappiness, no matter how much he tried to hide it. They often, without warning, would jump up on his lap and begin stroking his face, as if they already sensed something was not right with their granddad. He worried that it may not be a genuine display of affection, that, it was more out of pity, and he did not want them to feel obliged to deal with his 'baggage.'

He feared their pity for him would rob them of their childhood innocence, something that was painfully familiar to him. Yet, he valued their natural spontaneity and wanted to preserve it for as long as possible and did not want others to see him as a victim. Up to now, he had always managed to protect them from learning about his past trauma, but the only person who was suffering, was himself. He had reached a point in his life that he had more to lose by not changing. It was clear that family meant everything to him, and he was willing to try anything.

OPENING OLD WOUNDS

As John was already in a negative, hypnotic 'trance-like' state, it was a smooth process to gain access to his subconscious mind and begin the process of 'de-hypnotising' him.

But first, I had to 'anchor' him to a place in his mind where he could feel secure and if at any point during the therapy, he felt anxious, he could find his own way back to feeling relaxed and safe. He chose to think of his grandchildren, and I could tell he was already in his safe place when he instantly smiled as he recalled images of their innocent little faces, just as he had previously described.

I was aware that John had not just endured psychological trauma, he had also experienced physical abuse, so I used an indirect approach to suggest he would be able to relax the muscles in his body, in a way that was right for him, and whenever he felt ready, in his own time. Fortunately, this approach was met without any resistance, which can often happen unconsciously, when the person has experienced any form of abuse or coercive control, that could put them in a vulnerable position. Even though John was used to being told what to do and how to conform in the institution, I wanted to access the part of him that wanted to feel free to express his true self and for him to discover what that would feel like for him.

Negotiating was a skill that John was familiar with in his profession as a design engineer, so we began to explore the distinct parts of himself to find a solution that was right for him.

In John's case, I focused on his internal conflict and how he was communicating with himself using different 'Ego States,' Adult, Child, and Parent, according to an approach by a prominent psychiatrist, Dr. Eric Berne, who created transactional analysis (TA).

> Note;
>
> Every time we say or do something, there is a transaction taking place between ourselves and others. The basic premise is that people can change, and we all have a right to be in the world and be accepted, reinforcing the idea that everyone is valuable and has the ability for positive change and personal growth.

This is a skill I often teach my clients when there are struggling with conflicting emotions. The intention is to put things into perspective and assign structure to our thoughts.

I have outlined this as follows:

Parent Ego State stands for recordings of external events seen and experienced by a child up to the first five years of life. These recordings are accepted as fact and not questioned by the child.

Child Ego State stands for all recordings of internal events, feelings or emotions that are directly associated to external events, saw by the child up the first five years of life

Adult Ego State is the period in which a child develops the ability to perceive and understand situations that are different from what is seen (Parent) or felt (Child).

John was now ready to explore each of his Ego States with a view to developing awareness and trust in his own ability to view his life with a more balanced and wholesome perspective.

Reconnecting with his 'Child' Ego State, he was able to revisit the scared, vulnerable part of him that had endured years of trauma and abuse from an early age. While in a hypnotic trancelike state, John had the opportunity to return to his past and experience the emotional pain once again. But, this time, it was different, he had skills now that he never had previously. Familiarising himself with his 'Parent' Ego State came naturally to him as he quickly and effortlessly was able to use his own resources as a parent to soothe his own inner child.

One key role of the 'Parent' is to confirm stored information. Although, I could tell that John was visibly upset, it was also a bittersweet moment for him as he began exhaling deeply and sobbing spontaneously. He was able to allow his body to process all the pent-up stress it was holding for many years. Guided by his breath, his sympathetic nervous system was beginning to reset itself.

The 'Adult' Ego State serves as a 'data processor' that uses information from all three 'Ego States,' to put things into perspective and arrive at a decision. In John's case, he needed to remind himself of how far he had come in life, how much he had achieved, not just in material wealth, but how abundant his life had become, despite his traumatic experiences.

John's relaxed body and facial expressions needed no words. Judging by the number of times he exhaled deeply, it was clear to see that his body was releasing stress naturally and effortlessly. After the hypnotic trance, he said that he felt a huge weight had been lifted off him, and it was replaced with, what he described as, a feeling of finally 'coming home.'

When he was integrating, or bringing together, 'parts' of himself, under hypnosis, he said he recognised the various parts, but was unable to make the connections by himself. He realised, that in his effort to survive, he had not only detached himself from the pain but also the ability to feel any pleasure.

He had built a fortress strong enough to keep himself safe, but had unwittingly imprisoned himself from allowing others in. It was then he realised, forgiveness was something he gave as a gift to himself, to experience real freedom.

"Violence begets violence; hate begets hate.
And toughness begets a greater toughness.
It is all a descending spiral,
and the end is destruction — for everybody.
Along the way of life, someone must have enough sense
and morality to cut off the chain of hate."

-Martin Luther King Jr.

DRIVING CONTROLS

Darkness cannot drive out darkness,
only light can do that.
Hate cannot drive out hate,
only love can do that."~ Martin Luther King, Jr.

SIXTEEN-YEAR-OLD JASON SHOWED ALL the signs, at least on the outside, of being a 'tough guy'. He did not attempt to hide the fact he did not want to be 'fixed' by any therapist and was certainly not in agreement with talking to a stranger about his anger.

As far as he was concerned, this way of communicating had served him fine up until now. He just wished everyone in his family would back off and stop picking on him all the time. He only agreed to therapy because his parents warned him if he did not get his anger under control, then he would have to leave the family home. Jason's mother had already reached out to me in desperation as she was at her wit's end about his explosive temper. She explained that she and her husband were both living in fear of his unpredictable outbursts.

The entire family was affected by his aggressive behaviour which they found extremely distressing. His mother explained, embarrassingly, how Jason was not only verbally abusive but also physically threatening towards his siblings including breaking household valuables during his uncontrollable rages.

He was completely unmanageable, and they were afraid of what he might do next. He had always been quick-tempered when he was a child but now despite the fact he is fully grown, he still showed signs of emotional immaturity.

WALKING ON EGGSHELLS

Everyone who came into contact with Jason was walking on eggshells in the event he would get triggered and erupt into one of his explosive rages. They wondered where they went wrong.

As I opened my door to Jason, my first impressions were, somewhere inside him, was a frightened little boy. He had shielded himself behind his parents, making it clear to me, he didn't want to be seen. He appeared rigid and expressionless, and I could tell he was not happy about meeting me. Nevertheless, I wanted to find a way to connect with him, so I offered him a welcoming smile as I invited him in, ignoring any obvious signs of resistance in him.

As his eyes wandered around the walls in my office, he made every attempt to appear detached and disinterested as he did his best to maintain his 'tough-guy' stance, avoiding eye contact with me. I looked at him directly and said, "you don't want to be here, do you?" He nodded in agreement.

Then I said, "you're only here because your parents want you to be here, right?" and again he nodded. At least we agreed on something.

I hold the belief that there is nothing 'wrong' with my clients. I am more interested in what happened to them to cause their suffering. I became curious about his story, so I distracted him by asking him if he liked cars. I wanted to cause a sense of confusion in him, just enough to bypass his critical analytical mind. He looked at me and nodded. I saw this as an opportunity to explore the possibility of communicating with his subconscious mind.

BREAKING BARRIERS

Often, I come across someone who is resistant to change, and I find storytelling to be a powerful tool to break through the barriers put up by the conscious mind.

I began by telling him a story about the time I used to drive a Triumph Spitfire sports car. It really stood out and anytime I took it out for a run, it attracted many admiring glances since it was such a great-looking car, and even better when the rooftop was down. I described it as being an amazing experience to be able to drive that car. How I was able to handle the steering wheel as I negotiated sharp bends on the road. The feeling of my foot on the accelerator pedal and I listened to the sound of a powerful engine revving up, ready to take me wherever I wanted to go. Now, *that* was freedom.

I noticed a slight smile appear on Jason's face as I was reliving my experience. His eyes glazed over in a trancelike stare as he hung on my every word. I knew then his subconscious mind was activated, creating the images I was describing through his own internal filters. I wondered what he was thinking about, so I asked him, if he could have any car, what would it be?

He slowly raised his head and answered me with a half-smile. Then, he blurted out. "The Jaguar Project 8".

I didn't have any idea what he was talking about, but it didn't matter, I was more interested in getting him to engage his subconscious mind and expand his awareness. I wanted him to continue, so, I asked him what was so special about that Jaguar, and according to his knowledge, it was the fastest Jaguar ever built.

Now that Jason was willing to communicate with me at this level, I continued to encourage him with questions, like, what type of engine was installed in the Jaguar and if he could describe the interior what it would look like. I wanted to know how fast it could go. I was genuinely interested in cars and wanted to appear authentic and sincere. Jason, himself, was revved up at this point, (no pun intended) and what followed was an outpouring of technical information that held me captivated and wanting to hear more from him.

SLOWING DOWN

As I remained fixated on his every word, I noticed the tone in his voice changing, becoming softer, less curt. His face became more animated as he described the engine's ability to go from 0-60mph in just 3.3 seconds. He described the interior as if he were experiencing being inside the car at that moment. He appeared to be enjoying our 'chat' about cars. So, I asked him if he was able to drive a car and whether he held a driver's license. He reluctantly admitted he hadn't passed his driver's test yet but added that it was something he really wanted to do. Again, he lowered his head as the reality of being completely dependent on his parents hit home.

He left out a sigh as he looked down at his feet as his hands were twisting and turning, once again, he fell silent with his own thoughts. He looked helpless, and I knew I needed to find a way to generate 'mind tools' to help empower him, so he could feel that he had some level of control over his emotions.

'Conversational hypnosis,' guided by my curious tone of voice, drove him to imagine himself behind the wheel of the 'Jaguar 8,' right at this moment, with that monstrous engine and all that power. As his eyes were darting back and forth as his mind was processing my words, I asked him if he could imagine what might happen, if he were unable to master the controls. He was beginning to realise that this wasn't just a chat about care engines.

At some point, he began to discover it was more to do with himself and his inability to control his anger. He lowered his head as his eyes veered downward. He appeared calmer and more relaxed as he looked in my direction, but he still seemed lost.

DISENGAGING FEARS

Just then, he closed his eyes. It was like he had 'checked out' and didn't want to have to think. I became silent in that moment and wanted to meet him wherever he was right then. I told him it was ok, not to have to think about anything. In fact, it was better to let go of any need to think of thoughts at all and the part of him that was tired of trying to figure out how to control his feelings could just take a break and do nothing. I then suggested that he may feel more comfortable allowing his eyes to remain closed. When he heard my words, he began to sigh heavily, like his body was releasing all the stress that had been stored for a long time, for whatever reason.

I offered him suggestions to release, relax and let go of any need to hang on to whatever was not serving him in his life right now.

Suddenly, tears began to flow, as he started sobbing inconsolably. I asked him what was happening, and he uttered, "grandad Joe." I encouraged him to tell me about his grandad, and it was like a release of stored memories that had suddenly come flooding back to him.

He began to tell me how, when he was a child, he used to spend a lot of time in his grandad's workshop watching him fix things. He recalled a time when they built a go-cart. They both spend hours and hours putting it together. It was a labour of love between the two of them and the excitement and anticipation of seeing it finished is something he will never forget. Grandad Joe showed him how to steer the go-cart and insisted on him wearing a crash helmet, which wasn't so cool, but he didn't care since he felt so happy back then.

I wanted to focus on Jason's' strengths and direction in life, whether he had any hopes and dreams. I was curious to know what experiences had brought him to become so angry with the people closest to him. I wondered why memories of his grandad had brought him to tears.

He told me that when he was about 10 years old, during his school holidays, he was getting ready to go on a camping trip for the weekend. It was all planned, just him and grandad, Joe. He was looking forward to spending time with him going fishing and doing their usual outdoor pursuits.

Then a phone call changed everything. He knew by the sound of his mother's voice as she took the call that something was wrong. He could hear his mother crying and his father trying to comfort her. Grandad Joe had unexpectedly passed away in his sleep during the night.

All Jason remembers were the whisperings and furtive glances from various family members and he felt shocked and confused. He had never experienced anything like this before.

He described it as an overwhelming sense of heaviness in his body and he just froze, unable to feel anything. It was too much for his brain to process at the time and so, he pushed it aside, until now. He remembers his father telling him to 'man up' and not to be such a weakling and that the men in the family must show they are emotionally strong, and that crying was seen as a sign of weakness. His sister was allowed to cry and be emotional and he hated that. He wanted her to stop being so stupid and selfish.

As time went on, Jason became more distant and isolated from others and withdrew more into himself. It felt safer there. His mother tried to hide her grief about the loss of her father as she didn't want to upset her little boy by talking about it. Jason didn't want to mention his grandad for fear of upsetting his mother and so no one talked about the loss of such an important and well-loved member of their family. Everyone thought they were doing the right thing and handling their grief in the best way possible, but it just made matters worse.

The unexpressed sadness and feelings of loss had no outlet. Jason knew something was not right within himself, but he couldn't say what it was. Trivial things started to bother him, and he found himself becoming irritated at the slightest thing. He became easily triggered and quick tempered, feeling, as he described it, an uncontrollable urge to smash or break something. He knew he was frightening the people he was closest to, but he couldn't control himself. It was like a rush of fire racing through his body, and he couldn't stop it once it took hold of him. Instead of feeling strong, his behaviour left him feeling ashamed and weak, the very thing he wanted to avoid. His anger had taken over his life, and he didn't know who he was anymore. He did not like himself very much and he was tired of being controlled by his emotional triggers and wanted relief. It was obvious that Jason needed to find a way to channel and release the energy of pent-up anger, that he was holding in his body.

RELEASING THE CLUTCHES OF GRIEF

He needed to find a way to let go of the fear and grief he was holding on to and allow it to flow through him without any physical, mental, or emotional exertion. To achieve this outcome, Jason needed to find a way to express himself in an assertive rather than a reactive way if he were to enjoy the control and freedom he wanted.

By setting the intention of releasing the fear he was holding onto and focusing his attention towards attracting a higher vibration of peace, he could begin the process to heal old wounds from his past. Freedom begins with choices. Learning how to raise his vibration, requires a level of curiosity about everything that enters his personal space.

Jason realised he had never questioned why he was angry most of his adult life. When we explored his inability to express himself, with 'curious compassion' and without judgment, it was like a dam bursting its riverbanks. He started to sob uncontrollably as he remembered having to hold in all his pain and grief when his Grandad died. He was only 10 years old.

As Jason was able to reconnect with years of trapped or unexpressed grief and sadness, he finally understood that his anger was his way of releasing all that pent-up energy. His explosive tempers were the only way he knew how to cope, but they only brought him temporary relief. The aftermath of his outbursts had devastating consequences not only for himself, but for anyone who crossed his path.

During the course of a number of sessions, we explored ways of developing a new communication style to enable him to express himself without feeling overwhelmed or 'out of control,' and to give him the results that worked best for him.

RESPONSIBLE CHOICES

Jason liked the idea of having a sense of freedom to choose his own thoughts. Taking responsibility for making his own choices, allowed him to gain a feeling of inner strength and control. He could now make a decision to remember all the good times he enjoyed with his Grandad and to see how fortunate he was to have had experienced adventure and fun with him. This made him realise too, how much he was valued and loved by him.

The outcome for Jason was very positive, as he went ahead and completed a course of driving lessons, passed his test, and had already applied for his driver's license. He rediscovered his love of the outdoors, purchased a pair of hiking boots and had taken up fishing again. While engaging in these activities, he felt a close connection with his grandad and gained a new perspective, as a grown adult.

As all the positive memories came flooding back to him, he could now understand how Grandad loved the outdoors so much, and he felt a great sense of appreciation for what he had learned from him.

Jason developed a new level of self-awareness that had allowed him an opportunity to see how grandad lived his life in a way that matched his values. By continuing to follow in his footsteps, it was his way of honouring his memory.

> Life has, and will continue to challenge us, and it is not the event but our response to the event that matters in how we handle ourselves. We are also free to choose how we react in

any given situation, no matter how tough, and we can be the directors of our own lives.

'All the world's a stage, and we are all merely players' ~ William Shakespeare.

PULLING HER HAIR OUT

"When a person realises, they have been deeply heard, their eyes moisten. I think in some real sense they are weeping for joy. It is as though they were saying, "Thank God, somebody heard me. Someone knows what it's like to be me" ~ Carl R. Rogers

---

VERA WAS A QUIET, polite, softly spoken fifteen-year-old student who had been unintentionally pulling her hair out which left her with unsightly bald patches all over her head. I could tell by her shy mannerisms that she was struggling to engage with the basic level of communication skills.

Her mother seemed kind and caring and made no attempt to hide the fact she was worried about her daughter. She explained how she, herself, was at her wits end and that Vera attended numerous counselling sessions, but nothing was working to stop the habit of pulling her hair out. She was puzzled as to why this was happening since she considered her family to be incredibly united and happy.

As far as she was concerned, everyone got on well and it was a complete mystery. They wondered whether the behaviour was due to the stress of exams, which would have been expected, and this was partly true, but there was something else going on and I wasn't sure, yet, what it was.

A VOICE UNHEARD

I wondered why Vera had little to say, like she was lost for words, but I couldn't help noticing her body language was communicating more than she had realised. She appeared to be holding something back as she fidgeted with her hands and repeatedly tapped her foot on the floor. She kept looking across the room towards her mother with a look that could be only interpreted as a plea for assistance in explaining her predicament. I was curious about why she wanted her mother to explain what she was experiencing.

At this point, it was more important that Vera felt safe, so I respected her wishes. I was prompted, in this case, to use an approach by Carl Rogers, and offered her 'unconditional positive regard' to allow her an opportunity to feel heard.

The 6 Core Conditions of this approach are as follows:

1. Respect for another person.
2. Being non-judgmental and impartial.
3. Valuing a person and accepting them as a unique individual.
4. Acceptance of another person and their views, opinions, and beliefs.
5. Nurturing and caring for another person and being conscious of their needs.
6. Being compassionate and understanding a person's personal struggle with issues and problems.

Vera's mother explained to me that she had isolated herself from her friends because she was ashamed of how she looked. She was aware of people staring at her and imagined they were talking about her behind her back. She kept repeating how she looked like a freak and hated herself. She spent most of her time locked away in her bedroom so she wouldn't have to deal with the whisperings and curious looks from others.

In desperation, she brought Vera to a wig clinic to learn ways to disguise the bald patches. It was no good, she couldn't hide the devastating effects of her impulsive urges.

The second time I saw Vera, she appeared more relaxed, and I noticed her 7-year-old brother had accompanied them. I chatted to him briefly and he was well mannered and friendly. His mother brought him into the waiting room as he settled down to watch his favourite TV program. This gave me an opportunity to spend time alone with Vera. This time, she appeared to be more open to interacting with me.

GETTING A GRIP

I was curious to explore how her behaviour was affecting her, from her own perspective. She told me that most of the time she doesn't even realise she was doing it. She explained that it felt like she went into a 'trance-like' state, as she began pulling at her hair, and she was not satisfied, until she felt an intense burning sensation on her scalp. There was no thought of consequences at this point, it had now become an unconscious urge. She was completely unaware of what she was doing, and before she realised it, her hands were filled with bunches of her hair. As she uttered the words, tears rolled down her face. The automatic compulsion had taken over her life and she felt powerless. Her expression was blank and emotionless.

BREAKING THE SILENCE

She had already told me earlier that she had a passion for studying and learning, and it was important for her to do well and succeed in life. I was curious to learn more, as a way to redirect her focus away from her problems and more towards the solution, so I asked her about what she wanted to do as a career. She said she had hoped to study medicine or get a science degree, so we chatted for a while about that. She appeared to relax and was happy to open up and talk some more. Then, I casually commented on her little brother, and I remarked on how he appeared to be so charming and cute. She agreed, but I noticed a look on her face that prompted me to explore further and wondered what she wasn't saying. I knew by her body language that there was something bothering her and I wanted to find out what she was hiding.

As with any unconsciously driven habit, the place to find answers would be in the subconscious part of the mind. I began using hypnosis and suggestions to relax her body with breath-work and guided imagery. I led her to a place of comfort and safety within her own imagination, to access her hidden or repressed emotions, with the intention of getting to the root cause of her pain. Since studying was something that she enjoyed, I suggested she connect to the 'student part' of herself and imagine all the positive feelings that she experienced while studying in the privacy of her bedroom.

GUILTY SECRET UNVEILED

Then suddenly, the calmness soon turned into agitation as her thoughts were directed more towards the reality of the circumstances around her pain. I could see she was struggling to say something and encouraged her to share what was going on inside her head. She said she felt guilty about saying anything as she thought it would indicate that she was a bad person. I assured her that whatever it was, it could not be any worse than what she was already suffering which resulted in her pulling out her hair. What could be more painful I wondered? Why was she feeling so guilty?

While still in a light hypnotic trance and her conscious analytical mind temporarily suspended in time, the truth came pouring out. She revealed that when she was attempting to concentrate on her studies, her little brother would often burst into her bedroom excitedly, waving a paper airplane, jumping on her bed, making loud noises, and mimicking the sound of aircraft engines. She would tell him to leave but he would take no notice of her, and despite her pleas, he carried on relentlessly, continuing to ignore her. She would often resort to calling her mother to intervene to try and get him to calm down, but she was told to leave him alone, that he was only being friendly and didn't mean any harm.

Since she was eight years older than her brother, Vera felt she should be more protective over him and often felt bad about not being able to be more mature about it. She tried desperately to concentrate on her studies and ignore his antics, as the frustration continued to build inside her head to the point, she couldn't take it anymore. She would then feel a compulsion to grip her hair with her fists in a bid to relieve the tension and for a few moments, she could only feel the intense physical burning sensation on her scalp. She didn't know what else to do and nobody was taking her seriously. She wanted to explode in anger, but learned from past experiences, that there was no point in complaining.

NO ONE IS LISTENING

Her parents believed her brothers' stunts were hilarious, and she had always been told to leave him alone. She admitted that she felt resentful and angry and didn't like herself for feeling this way. Afterwards, she would become ashamed of her thoughts and feelings. She believed that if her parents found out about how she really felt, she was sure they wouldn't be impressed with her. As a result, she learned that it was better to push her feelings to the back of her mind and ignore them.

Unwittingly, Vera had created an even bigger problem for herself. There was a constant battle being fought inside her head and she believed she needed to be punished for thinking badly about her brother and her parents. She tried to tell herself that he was only an innocent child who just wanted to have fun and do the typical 'rough and tumble' boy stuff. He wanted everyone to look at how good he was, with all his antics, as he entertained the whole family. He relished in all the positive attention he was getting.

Meanwhile, she continued to struggle with her internal dialogue, that nagging voice in her head as she began to question herself. She wondered how could she be so horrible to try and spoil his fun, or to be responsible for ruining any pleasure he brought to her parents. She had always been a 'good girl' and never caused anyone any problems, now she was fussing over something so trivial. The thoughts went round and round in her head, in a loop, and no matter how much she didn't want to have those thoughts, the more obsessive and intense they became. The problem was beyond her control.

SHAME ON ME

The body never lies and will always find a way to express emotional pain. In this case, Vera did not have the cognitive skills to help herself. According to her, she found herself in a hopeless situation where she had no control over her external environment. The self-loathing, guilt, and shame, to her, seemed justified for harbouring negative thoughts about her brother. The resentment and frustration towards her parents for their lack of support and understanding, was too much for her to bear. As she began inflicting pain on herself by pulling her hair out, she could feel her pain in a physical form.

This distorted, irrational activity was her way of seeking some form of retribution and relief at the same time. This sounds like a contradiction and may not appear to make any sense, but none of this unconscious behaviour is created in a logical way. Even though the act of pulling her hair out was causing her a lot of physical pain, the alternative was much worse. It provided her a distraction away from having to deal with a situation that appeared hopeless. She did not know what else to do, she could not stop it. The behaviour, when performed repeatedly, turned into a habit that dominated her entire life.

By the time she had come to see me, she had reached a stage she was no longer aware of her repetitive actions of pulling out her hair. The habit was now running on automatic pilot, she had learned to normalise the behaviour and had almost given up hope of ever overcoming it.

> Note: 'Trichotillomania,' as this behaviour is called, is not something that can be rationalised by the conscious mind. Every negative behaviour has a 'secondary gain,' which meant that the part of her mind that was unable to process the emotional pain, had produced a way to solve the problem, even though the consequences were unhelpful or destructive.

Most interactions with clients would not always allow me the opportunity to explore the nature of relationships between family members, but in this case, I was fortunate to have had that opportunity. Vera was open to whatever would bring her relief and I assured her that I would handle it with the utmost respect for her and her mother. There would be no blame games or playing hide and seek, unlike her little brother, it was time to unveil the truth.

UNDERSTOOD

When vera's mother became aware of her daughter's dilemma with her brother and her feelings of being unheard and invalidated, she was flabbergasted. She thought it was normal sibling behaviour. Nevertheless, she continued to refer to her son's charming personality, that is, until Vera started to cry. There was a deafening silence in the room where no one spoke. No words could communicate the obvious distress that was being expressed by Vera. It was then that her mother began to listen with a more serious demeanour as she sat upright to focus on what her daughter had to say. She had not realised how deeply it had affected her as she listened with obvious intention to understand whatever it was that she needed to hear. The floodgates had already opened and it was the perfect opportunity for Vera to reveal how she really felt. I encouraged her to open up and share her thoughts in a safe environment and reassured her that whatever she revealed, it would be for positive intentions. Vera embarrassingly explained how she felt bad for complaining about her brother since she knew he didn't mean any harm. She reminded her mother about his boisterous antics and admitted she couldn't help feeling overwhelmed while she was trying to concentrate on her studies. Her mother was very sympathetic and open to any suggestions at this point. It was nobody's fault and there were no bad intentions, just a lack of communication and misunderstandings all round.

We, therefore, unanimously agreed that her brother should not be aware of the detrimental effects of his behaviour on his sister, since his intention was not to harm anyone. The fact that his antics did not bother any other members of the family, had no relevance on the fact that Vera's experience was unique to her. It was her reality, and that was all that mattered, since she was the one pulling her hair out.

Now that the awareness was out in the open, there was no more room for shame and guilt. Vera was able to process all of her bottled-up emotions and she received positive reassurance of a better style of communication and understanding in the future.

In further sessions, she learned how to recognise her triggers that led to her compulsion for pulling her hair. We also explored new, healthier ways to substitute her old patterns of behaviour. She continued to write a daily journal of her thoughts and feelings as a channel to help release some of her anxiety and worry. It was agreed that her parents would assume the responsibility for her brother's behaviour to relieve any further pressure on her. She eventually learned to accept herself and recognise what was within her control and what was not her responsibility.

The 'compulsion' had run its course when the need that it served was met with more powerful rewards. This was achieved using high intensity neuro linguistic programming (NLP), combined with post hypnotic suggestions of a future version of herself. The treatment continued 'until' her subconscious mind was willing to negotiate precise details of how it would accept the new 'terms and conditions'.

"Only when you observe with the intent to understand you will discover the deeper truth. Having someone who listens is a gift, but to be truly heard, is a real treasure." ~Tatjana Urbic

HOME IS WHERE THE HEART IS

SELINA WAS AN ATTRACTIVE, well-groomed lady in her late 50's and although she appeared casual, she was well-coordinated with her unique style of dressing. She moved with a confident stride and her warm smile was somewhat misleading. I began to wonder how I could help her, but as soon she sat down, it became glaringly obvious why she had come to see me. Her posture had suddenly become guarded and rigid, and the look on her face left me in no doubt that something was troubling her. I asked her what brought her to seek my help, and she commenced by clearing her throat. I could see she was struggling to get her words out when she finally admitted that she didn't know who she was anymore and muttered something about feeling lost and confused. I encouraged her to tell me more to help me understand and be able to assess the extent of her problem.

She told me she worked as a recruitment consultant for small businesses, and she loved her job. She admitted that she felt respected and appreciated by her work colleagues who often looked to her for advice, not just on work-related issues but they also trusted her enough to confide in her on private matters.

I noticed Selina's facial expression changed again as she became slightly anxious and hesitant, but I beckoned her to continue. It has been said that the body never lies, and in her case, it appeared to be crying out for help. She told me that her personal life was a disaster and she said she felt like a hypocrite and a fake as she provided support to everyone around her, while she was drowning in her conflicting thoughts and emotions.

Outside of work, she always felt uncomfortable mingling in groups and struggled to make conversation. Most of the time she felt like she didn't belong anywhere, always observing from a distance, but never participating fully. As she distanced herself, she would watch others talking naturally and seemingly without effort, causing her to experience a crippling sense of isolation and loneliness. She tried so hard to fit in, but she always felt a bit 'different' in a weird sort of way, and never really felt at ease with herself. It was as if she was rehearsing a part in a play. All this pretence was exhausting, trying to figure out how to play the game of surviving and constantly having to be on guard. Her shy, avoidant behaviour attracted unwanted attention and it was becoming glaringly obvious that others were noticing it. It seemed like there was no escape and nowhere for her to hide.

Her Story

Growing up, she was an obvious target for bullies since she was unable to hide her awkward shyness. Because of this, some of her schoolteachers made attempts to toughen her up by asking her what was 'wrong' with her and why she didn't mix well with the other kids in the school playground.

She remembers one particular incident when her only friend was off sick from school. The teacher on duty had noticed that she was standing by herself, watching others playing together. Before long, Selina suddenly felt her arm being pulled, as she was ushered along and forced to run around the school building, as the teacher led her by the arm the entire time. It was like a scene from the Pied Piper. Everyone was encouraged to join in, presumably to create a sense of comradery. She will never forget the humiliation and embarrassment when all the children began laughing at her.

On returning to the classroom, Selina began sobbing uncontrollably, she was upset to the extent that she could hardly catch her breath. Her chest felt tight. She was terrified. The teacher didn't expect this level of response from her and tried to get her to snap out of it by calling her a 'big baby'. Then everyone started to snigger and whisper when the teacher continued to put pressure on her to stop crying. But it only made matters worse, and as the classroom fell silent, Selina felt isolated and alone. The only memory she had regarding that incident, was when her mother, on hearing about the devastating effect it had on her, went to the school, and insisted on an apology from the teacher. Unfortunately, Selina was still too distressed to accept it. But one thing she will always remember was how her mother took the time to listen to her, and to stand up for her. She felt it was important enough not to ignore.

Unstable Roots

Selina was the eldest girl from a family of eight and would often assume the role of minder to her younger siblings. Her parents appeared to have been in permanent conflict about raising the children. There were no house rules or structured mealtimes, it was often disorganised chaos. She remembers always cleaning and tidying the house, not because it was expected of her, but she was not comfortable having her surroundings in such a disordered state. This didn't allow her much free time for anything else, although she did enjoy painting and drawing and found it gave her the means to detach from reality. She would often find herself daydreaming for significant periods and she became accustomed to living in her own little bubble. Her mother was also a dreamer for as long as she can remember, and she could never recall engaging in any meaningful conversations with her. Selina soon learned not to bother her too much, since she appeared to have had enough troubles of her own. Looking back on it now, she wondered whether her mother may have been suffering from depression.

Her father was a strong presence in the house. He was full of fun and laughter and it was clear he cared a lot for all of the children and wanted them to do well in life. Both parents had the best intentions for the family, unfortunately, they were unable to sort out their differences and got lost in the trials and tribulations of life. The consequences of this were neglect and abandonment and sadly, the children paid the price. During those unpredictable times, the heavy burden of responsibility for doing housework, looking after her younger siblings, along with her studies, often left Selina experiencing feelings of hopelessness and despair, as she saw no end to her predicament.

Angel in Disguise

Then she met Priscilla, who was one of the most popular girls in the school. She had sensed Selina's shy nature and made every effort to make her feel included. She would share her lunch with her when she noticed that Selina didn't have a packed lunch on a particular day. Soon, a friendship developed between them when they discovered they had mutual interests in art and music, and they also shared a similar sense of humour.

Selina was happy she had met someone who took an interest in her and cared about her wellbeing. This friendship appeared to be just what she needed to help her overcome her insecurities and feelings of not being 'good enough.' As they began to spend more time together, they became more like siblings than friends. This soon progressed to overnight stays at Pricilla's house as their friendship grew stronger and Selina had practically become part of their family. She finally began to feel safe and secure and thought to herself that this is what a 'normal' family is supposed to be like. She found herself forming an attachment to Priscilla's family and gradually, over time, becoming more detached from her own family.

Other Attachments

Priscilla's mother enjoyed listening to her stories and general chit-chat. She remembers engaging in lengthy, meaningful conversations while sitting by an open fire and enjoying a cup of comforting hot cocoa as they laughed for hours on end. It was refreshing to know that someone was interested in listening to her. Selina soon developed a close bond with Priscilla's mother, and she was so grateful for the attention and kindness showed to her, that she willingly helped in the kitchen, preparing food for their family. Priscilla would often be in another room playing the piano or listening to music. She was accepted as part of their family and, most importantly, she felt safe.

However, the more time she spent away from home, often for weeks at a time, she began to realise that all was not as it seemed in Priscilla's home life either. There was disharmony and tension of another kind, which left her wondering if she had overestimated the solidity of their family, in an attempt to clutch at some semblance of 'normality.' Selina did not wish to disclose any additional information about what she had observed within her friend's family dynamics. She felt it would be a form of betrayal or ingratitude for the kindness shown to her at a vulnerable time in her life. She had chosen to ignore anything other than the many positive experiences she had from the age of 10 to around 16 years. I acknowledged and respected her decision.

Family Values

After hearing Selina's story, it became clear why she was compelled to seek security and safety elsewhere, and because she didn't grow up in a secure environment throughout most of her childhood years, she had a very vague sense of self. The only memories she had of her earlier years, were her attempts to hide, and seek refuge from the dramas in her home. She would often use humour which often helped create a distraction from feelings of fear and insecurity. She tried to be a good person, to do the right thing, in the hope of creating a harmonious environment, and consequently became a people pleaser, to the point of losing her sense of self. She didn't know who she was supposed to be and learning to self-regulate was a constant challenge for her. She described it like a sailboat drifting in the ocean, without a rudder.

I could see that Selina was unable to hide her sadness and as her story unfolded. It became clear to me that family and security were important to her, but it was obvious that the relationship she had with herself needed more immediate consideration.

Trauma Bonding

Selina had developed survival skills while she navigated her way through the difficulties of her childhood. Searching for a sense of connection and security through other people was a constant void that was left unfilled. We explored certain behaviours that were working against her and needed to change if she was to achieve her goal of becoming content with her authentic self.

There are many theories as to why she developed her thoughts and beliefs that led her to choose the type of behaviours that caused her to feel anxious and avoidant in social settings. I will not go into the complexities of those theories, rather, how I helped her to overcome her challenges.

Throughout most of her life, Selina believed she was not 'good enough' and had unconsciously been drawn towards relationships that had a power imbalance.

She had formed unhealthy attachments, or 'trauma bonds' and would often tolerate mistreatment by others, but never found the courage to stand up for herself. This often left her feeling inadequate, unappreciated, and taken for granted.

As a self-confessed people pleaser, and in an effort to avoid conflict, she developed a behaviour that would work against her.

This avoidant behaviour worked well on one level by keeping her safe from predators, but it worked against her on another level, by keeping her isolated and alone.

Her protective barriers were created to keep out rejection and sadness, but she discovered it also kept out her joy.

Growing New Roots

Cognitive behavioural therapy (CBT) provided structure to her thoughts and beliefs and helped identify behavioural patterns, their consequences, both positive and negative and find alternative ways to manage her emotions. In order to change her belief around the meaning she associated with the word 'conflict', it was necessary to find a way to break the 'circuit' in her brain so she could see it in a completely different light.

We did this by her recognising her triggers regarding conflict and measuring the intensity of her emotions with each stimulus, using a SUDS scale (subjective units of distress). This allowed Selina to put her beliefs into perspective using the measurement which was proportionate to whatever event she was facing. She was then in a position to decide whether it was worth allowing herself to get triggered.

The 'silly persona' she created to distract from difficult experiences, unfortunately, had attracted a negative response of not being taken seriously, or worse, being mocked by others. We examined this 'silly' alter ego state she had developed and discovered that she liked that part of herself since it helped her overcome difficult occurrences. Laughter and fun were important to her and she didn't want to change it. In this case, we explored ways to manage the unhelpful responses from others. We succeeded in changing the meaning she attributed to the word 'silly' and reframed it to have a more positive association. This meant that she was able to view it as a character strength rather than a weakness. Over a few follow up sessions, we focused on building her confidence to embrace her fun part as she learned to appreciate herself more and give less attention to seeking the approval of others.

The ability to change the meaning she associated with her thoughts and in particular about herself, gave Selina a valuable tool that she could apply to every area of her life. She was beginning to develop a curiosity about how she could convert her past experiences into positive learnings. In this instance, I suggested she keep a journal on the pivotal moments in her life and put this new skill into practice to enable a positive transformation.

Based on the understanding that the past is gone and cannot be changed but using this technique of altering the meaning and associations to the events that happened, opens up a whole new world of possibilities.

As part of her healing journey, Selina assumed the probability that her parents were most likely victims of suffering themselves and couldn't be the sort of parents she would have wanted or envisaged. She did, however, gain some positive insights into her family history as she examined patterns and artistic talents that were passed down through generations.

Some of the challenging life experiences she endured could only be described as, flying without wings. She would be forever grateful to her 'surrogate' family who provided a safe place until she could find her own wings.

It was through the process of self-reflection that she came to realise that the lessons she learned throughout her life, made her stronger and more resilient, which consequently became the wind beneath her wings.

'Angels don't always have wings; they often lift us, so we can soar to even greater heights' ~ Unknown

I AM NOT MY STORY

To be or not to be…that is the question ~ *William Shakespeare*

I'M ALWAYS curious to unravel the mystery of how people translate their life experiences into a script, that then becomes their story. How do they come to believe, that once it is written, it somehow cannot be changed, even if the story is clearly causing immense suffering?

People often get stuck by repeating the same old story over and over, thus reinforcing it. Wishing things would change for the better is not going to work, while using the same behaviour that caused the problems in the first place.

Each of us has a story to tell and we want, above all, to be heard and understood. As humans, we want to feel connected and loved and feel that we matter in some way or another. And when this does not happen, it often throws us out of balance, often to the detriment of our health in many ways. The following 4 dimensions outline how we suffer.

On a **physical** level, we can get tension headaches, stomach pains, or suffer exhaustion.

On a **personal** level, feelings of not being enough, wondering what's wrong with me. Saying things like; I don't like myself, I'm useless.

On a **social** level, feeling disconnected, the odd one out, not belonging, feeling like an observer while watching others live their lives.

On a **spiritual** level, constantly searching for meaning and purpose in our lives.

The following story is about one woman's survival from trauma, from an unexpected source.

Jane was a wife, and mother to two adult children. She worked hard most of her life and survived many tough challenges.

Grief and loss were familiar burdens to her, and she had become accustomed to 'getting through' whatever challenges came her way. Entertaining thoughts of joy or happiness were considered by her to be an indulgence, and the furthest thing from her mind. She had learned to cope, but there was one thing bothering her and she wasn't sure how to deal with it. This brought her to seek my help.

Jane commented that she had conflicting feelings towards some of her close friends. They had always been supportive through the difficult times but for some reason, something changed, which left her confused.

She tried to piece together the sequence of events that led up to the present state of affairs. She started by telling me how she made a difficult decision to return to her studies and invest herself in a higher level of education. She had great expectations that her decision would allow her to become more independent and hopefully create a happier life than what she had experienced in her past.

Her training in mental health afforded her an opportunity to make a difference in helping others achieve a better quality of life. She knew she could contribute valuable, personal lived experiences.

This life changing decision meant spending many long hours immersed in books and attending lectures, which allowed little time for family, friends, and important celebratory events. Many sacrifices were made, driven by her desire and hope of creating a more fulfilling and meaningful life.

To her amazement, Jane achieved a standard of academic award far greater than she expected. This meant a lot to her, since, from an early age, she was aware that she was not the brightest in her class. She remembers been unable to concentrate fully and been reprimanded by teachers for her tendency to daydream and was often made fun of by her peers.

She was never diagnosed with any 'medical syndrome,' yet she muddled her way through her school years with a sense of frustration for being unable to figure out what was 'wrong' with her.

Because she was never formally diagnosed with any 'learning disability,' she found her own way to navigate through all the rules and regulations imposed on her by society's expectations of how she 'should' perform academically.

Finally, her years of challenging academic research studies paid off and she achieved what she set out to do. So, why wasn't she happy?

LIFTING THE VEIL OF TRUTH

Although, she graduated at honors level and was proud of her achievement, Jane had not expected a few of her friends to behave in the way they did. They appeared indifferent to the point of being dismissive.

She was met with a frosty response from the very people she expected to be happy for her. The only conclusion she could draw from their behaviour was that they hadn't expected her to succeed academically. It rocked their perception of her, as being a bit 'scatterbrained', and at every opportunity, they would remind her of it. There would often be the odd snide remark followed by an attempt to mask it as a joke. Despite feeling sad and deflated, she never questioned or acknowledged how much their behaviour had impacted her, until now.

On reflection, if the truth be told, they behaved like they always did, true to form. She said she felt like she had been asleep for a long time and suddenly woke up. She began to wonder whether she really knew herself at all. Since completing many hours of both personal and professional development, she was beginning to look at everyone and everything differently and what she discovered, was that she was being 'Gaslighted!'

> Note:
> This is a term used to describe when someone is being dismissed or invalidated and when the 'victim' of this abuse tries to defend themselves or question the abusive behaviour, it often gets masked as a joke. There is an implication that it is taken up the wrong way. This often leaves the victim confused and questioning their own sanity.

Jane had normalised this behaviour and had not recognised it for what it was, passive aggressive and covert bullying. When this new awareness of what she was being subjected to came to light, Jane began to feel unwell. Her body ached all over and her muscles became stiff and sore. She could barely speak, her throat hurt, her chest felt tight and she struggled to breathe. She was becoming angry and frustrated that her body had let her down. She was tired all the time, and all she wanted to do was sleep and not to be bothered by anyone.

She concluded that all her years of study and lack of sleep before exams must have taken its toll on her. She wondered, what was the point in learning how to offer help to others when she couldn't even take care of herself. She had hit rock bottom in every area of her life, and by the time Jane came to see me for help, I could tell from the initial consultation, that she was experiencing what is known as, 'an existential crisis.' She felt that her world was falling apart, and she didn't know who she was or what she wanted anymore.

She thought that by resting her physical body that it would somehow be enough, but there was still the unexpressed and unresolved emotional pain that she had not dealt with, yet. As she reflected on her life, it became clear to her that she had inadvertently taken on the 'persona' of the daydreaming, scatterbrained girl, who had then become her identity. It was how she portrayed herself to the outside world, yet it did not quite reflect her real self, whoever she was.

She remembered how she used to laugh her way through any challenges. It was how she coped, pretending that she was fine to avoid confrontation and conflict, but deep down, she knew she was hanging on by a thread. Now, that same thread had re-attached itself, and she needed to find a way to tie up those loose ends.

It was obvious to her that those past hurts had re-surfaced, and it was time to face the challenges that she had been avoiding, if she were to discover her true, authentic self.

Jane's story had always been based more on how others perceived her, rather than how she saw herself. Her unfulfilled expectations from others caused her to feel disappointed and dismissed as long as she measured her self-worth by the opinions of others. She knew she had to change if she wanted to experience true freedom and 'self-actualisation,' in other words, to become her 'authentic self.'

Using an 'Existential' approach, the focus of our sessions was based on 3 themes in relation to **Responsibility, Freedom** and **Meaning**

We looked at Jane's relationship with herself and others and explored ways in which she could assume *responsibility* for the choices she made in her life.

We examined her *freedom* to express herself without fear of being judged or seeking approval from external sources.

Finding *meaning* in her life required her to examine her core values, which were to help make a difference in the lives of others through her work.

Through our work together, Jane came to realise that she was responsible only for herself. She was able to recognise what *was* and *was not*, within her control, and make better decisions.

'Freedom is what you do with what has been done to you' ~ Jean-Paul Sartre

REWRITING MY STORY

Combining hypnosis and psychotherapy, together, we began to explore the conflicting emotions of fear and isolation, that she was struggling with, inside her mind. There were no complicated techniques used in this case. Jane already had all the answers to her problems and she was able to arrive at her own conclusions.

This new awareness offered her insight and understanding of what was really going on for her in many aspects of her life, and she realised she had choices. She no longer needed to 'react,' but could choose to 'respond' in a way that honoured her true values. She was gradually becoming comfortable with a more assertive version of herself and no longer felt like she was a victim.

One of the biggest lessons she learned during our sessions together was, that hurt people hurt others, and how people treat others, says more about the pain that exists within themselves.

Life is compared to a Stage, and this was her story; she played the lead part. She has become the script writer, and director of her own play.

"Between stimulus and response there is a space.
In that space is our power to choose our response.
In our response lies our growth and our freedom." ~Viktor Frankl

GROUNDING & HEALING ENERGY MEDITATION

Created by Me for You

FIND YOURSELF A COMFORTABLE POSITION, wherever you happen to be in this very moment....be there right now.

Set your intention to whatever you would like to experience, without judgment of how it will come about, trusting, that it will be right for you.

Take a moment to notice your breath, breathing in through your nose, as your stomach rises.

Do this for the count of 3, hold your breath for a second, then let it out through your nose, for the count of 5 as your stomach shrinks back down again. Repeat this process 4 more times

Allow your mind to wander and drift, and you may become aware that there are thoughts entering your head, just notice them passing through. Thoughts are thoughts, you don't need to act on a thought, sweep them away like they were never there, and then bring your attention back to your breath.

Now, imagine that there are roots reaching down from the soles of your feet, like the roots of a tree, going down deep into the ground, connecting you with the 'Universal Life-Force' of the female energy, 'Mother Earth,' grounding, supporting, and revitalising you.

Feel her powerful, nurturing energy circling back up through your feet, all the way up your legs and into your body, through an imaginary channel within you.

Allow it to spread in an outward flowing motion, filling every cell in your body with a wonderfully, soothing, healing sense of comfort.

Allow this same healing energy to wash away and clear any old unwanted thought-forms, or patterns of behaviour that do not serve you in your life right now.

Imagine, if you can, that you are having a deep cleansing shower on the inside.

Let that process happen now, all by itself, embracing this new lighter feeling swirling throughout your entire being, like you are floating on a white fluffy cloud of weightlessness.

Now, imagine the colour **green** as you tune into your heart space, opening to receiving positive vibrations, filling you with infinite abundance.

Visualise the colour **blue,** as you become aware of the area around your throat, and how it serves you in communicating with words and speaking your truth, honouring the person you are right now, accepting yourself, letting go of judgment.

See the colour **yellow**...as you imagine yourself basking in the warmth of the sun as it radiates towards you all the positive changes and new beginnings that are created for your highest good, bringing more joy and happiness into your life.

Now, see the colour **orange** when you breathe into your stomach, embracing your creativity and ability to express your emotions with ease, connecting you with the universal consciousness, bringing you greater clarity and awareness of yourself.

See the colour **red** as you begin to feel the change happening within you now, becoming filled with more confidence, courage, and stability in all your relationships.

Now tune in to the colour **purple** and to a higher vibrational frequency, creating a powerful alignment with your intuitive mind.

Becoming more present now and witnessing your thoughts…as you can observe how peaceful and calm your mind and body can become…when you just allow it to be.

Namaste,

Susan McElligott MA

FURTHER READING & VIEWING

Berne, E., 2011. Games People Play.

Berne, E., 2016. *Transactional analysis in psychotherapy*. Pickle Partners Publishing.

Bradshaw J., (1933-2016) The Family, Healing the Shame That Binds You, Homecoming, Creating Love, and Family Secrets.

Corey, G., Corey, M. and Muratori, M. (2010). *I never knew I had a choice*. 9th ed. Canada: Brooks/Cole.

Corydon Hammond D., "Handbook of Hypnotic Suggestions and Metaphors."

DBT Skills: Distress Tolerance & Crisis Survival. Accessed at: https://youtu.be/YeAMHacC8P8

Craig G., EFT Tapping for Anxiety, Stress Relief, How to Calm Anxiety Without Medication. Accessed at: https://youtu.be/zkm7No8z5V4.

The Tapping Solution. Accessed at: https://www.thetappingsolution.com

Diener, E. and Chan, M., (2011). *Happy People Live Longer: Subjective Well-Being Contributes to Health and Longevity*. Applied Psychology: Health and Well-Being, 3(1), pp.1-43.

Eger E., *The Choice*. Accessed at: https://youtu.be/Lr4JuvkfIKw

Erickson, M., 2000. *My Voice Will Go With You*. New York: Triangle Pr.

European Association of Professional Hypnotherapists(EAPH): https://eaph.ie

Existential Therapy Explained. Accessed at: https://youtu.be/YvAvc2aWup0

Frankl, V., 2000. Man's Search for Meaning. New York: Houghton, Mifflin.

Frankl, V., (2014). *"The Will to Meaning: foundations and applications of Logotherapy"*. Penguin

Gaslighting Explained. Accessed at: https://youtu.be/FISZshe9L3s

Hunter, R., 2005. Hypnosis for Inner Conflict Resolution. 1st ed. Bancyfelin: Crown House Publishing.

Hunter, C. and Eimer, B., 2012. The Art of Hypnotic Regression Therapy. 1st ed. Carmarthen: Crown House Publishing.

Joyce, P., 2018. *Skills in Gestalt Counselling & Psychotherapy*. [S.l.]: SAGE Publications Ltd.

Levine, A. and Heller, R., 2010. *Attached*. 1st ed.

https://nationalpsychologist.com/2015/05/using-hypnosis-with-children/102896.html

https://pedsinreview.aappublications.org/content/17/1/5

Maté, Gabor., (2019) When the Body Says No. 1st ed. Vermilion.

Maté, Gabor., (2021) How Childhood Trauma Leads to Addiction. Accessed at: https://youtu.be/BVg2bfqblGI

NLP: The Essential Guide to Neuro-Linguistic Programming. Hoobyar, T., Sanders, S. and Dotz, T., 2014. New York: William Morrow Paperbacks.

Nongard, R., 2011. Magic Words, the sourcebook of hypnosis patter and scripts. 1st ed. Lulu Com.

Nongard, R., 2012. Medical Hypnotherapy. 1st ed. Lulu Com.

O'Donohue, J., (1997). Spiritual Wisdom from the Celtic World. New York: Bantam Press.

Ramani, S Durvasula 2021. When being Gaslighted makes YOU seem unstable.

Accessed at: https://youtu.be/xI-VR6Pxrvc

Rogers, C., https://mick-cooper.squarespace.com/new-blog/2019/4/2/carl-rogerss-core-conditions-are-they-necessary-and-sufficient

Singer, M., 2011. *The Untethered Soul*. Old Saybrook, CT

Tahir, Irum.,(2015) How to change your limiting beliefs for more success. Accessed at: https://youtu.be/Fom14XGMFHA

Van der Kolk, B., 2015 The Body Keeps The Score. New York: Penguin Books.

Van der Kolk, B.,(2021) Healing Trauma and How the Body Keeps the Score.

Accessed at: https://youtu.be/d_YApSkqsxM

Van Deurzen, E., and Arnold-Baker, C., (2005). Existential Perspectives on Human Issues. Palgrave Macmillan

Printed in Great Britain
by Amazon